SCOTTISH

SKIING

The Golden Years 1950-1990

SCOTTISH
SKIING

The Golden Years 1950-1990

Ed Rattray

Matador
9 Priory Business Park
Kibworth Beauchamp
Leicestershire LE8 0RX, UK
Tel: (+44) 116 279 2299
Fax: (+44) 116 279 2277
Email: books@troubador.co.uk
Web: www.troubador.co.uk/matador

ISBN 978 1780880 372

British Library Cataloguing in Publication Data.
A catalogue record for this book is available from the British Library.

Typeset in 12pt Adobe Garamond Pro by Troubador Publishing Ltd, Leicester, UK
Printed and bound in the UK by TJ International, Padstow, Cornwall

Matador is an imprint of Troubador Publishing Ltd

To Louise

Introduction

Ed Rattray began climbing in the Cairngorms in the 1940s and first donned skis in 1950, long before modern equipment was available and when mountain clothing and skis were all ex-War Department kit. He graduated into the Etchacan and Cairngorm Mountaineering Clubs and became a founder member of the Aberdeen Ski Club in 1956. Later, he was active in helping to set up the Scottish National Ski Council in 1963 (now known as Snowsport Scotland). The skiing movement in Scotland burst into life as soon as the first major ski tows and lifts were built in 1961. He was just one of tens of thousands of skiers swept along by the euphoria of the time and it was the beginning of what he calls the skiing revolution.

Throughout the 1960s, when Scotland went skiing, more than a hundred clubs were formed while schools, youth organisations, and thousands of other individuals, discovered the winter mountains. From that movement, young Scottish athletes emerged and began to dominate in the sport to become British Alpine Skiing Champions and GB Olympic Team members. His involvement at club and national level over many years meant he amassed a large archive of information and pictures, which he uses to illustrate this, his historical interpretation of the last half of the last century. **The Golden Years of Scottish Skiing**. So, this book is part history, part memoir and part anecdote.

The author on the Italian side of the Vallee Blanche, below Mont Blanc

Chapter 1

Scotland Went Skiing

Snow addiction

There was a revolution in ski sport in Scotland and it began slowly in the 1950s, then exploded into the 1960s. The Golden Years were in the 1960s, through to the 1990s, when skiing became accessible and affordable for the masses. Ski clubs sprung up all around the country and the rush was on to build ski lifts and tows to satisfy the rapidly growing demand for uplift.

Going back in time, to the first half of the last century, skiing had been an elitist sport, enjoyed by the few who had the leisure time and the resources to travel and climb the winter mountains, or to take railway travel to the Alps. The Scottish Ski Club founded in 1907 had a modest membership in its early years and ceased to exist for several years during and after the First World War, when many members died.

By the 1930s its resurgence began and after the Second World War it grew steadily as the senior club in Scotland. It still is, having seen many other newer ski clubs emerge in the golden years between 1960 and 1990, flourish and blossom, only to disappear as the sport developed and the need for clubs grew less. In that later period the need for the basic services provided by over a hundred ski clubs were no longer needed. Club ski coach travel, for instance, went out as the motor car came in. Only the clubs which had strong training, racing or social programmes survived. Today, 34 clubs continue in Scotland and are affiliated to Snowsport Scotland, the National Body.

In the post war 1950s the first need was for club buses, for club ski hire facilities and basic ski tuition. The social element was there too, because there was nothing quite like a climber's or skier's bus on the way home from the hills to encourage folk to sing. By the 1970s the motor car slowly became the preferred mode of travel, affordable by more and more.

The country was upbeat. People had more leisure time, more disposable money and therefore wider horizons. Air travel became available and by the late 1970s far off places just began to be options for many more. There are thousands of "mature" skiers in Scotland today who will remember those golden days of the skiing revolution when snow lay on the mountains for months on end and the weekend rush to get to the ski slopes became an exodus from the cities and towns across the country. Today, if we do a head count at Scotland's main airports any Saturday from January till April, it is possible to estimate how many "mature" Scots now fly abroad to ski but who had their first taste of the sport on Scottish snow perhaps thirty or forty years ago.

As the lure of the snow mountains slowly gathered pace before World War II the Scottish Ski Club built shelter huts on Ben Lawers, (1214m) and Meall Gargh, (968m) in Highland Perthshire, while the Dundee Ski Club, which broke away from the Scottish and was founded in 1937, favoured Ben Gulabin, in Glenshee. After that war, Glencoe was an early focus of activity and in 1956 the Scottish Ski Club built the first ever fixed ski tow on Meall a' Bhuiridh. The Aberdeen Ski Club founded in 1956 adopted Carn an Tuirc (1019m) on the Braemar side of the infamous Devil's Elbow hill pass, with their first mountain hut followed by a diesel rope tow which was shared with the Scottish Ski Club. These clubs built the early ski tows, pioneered regular ski bus travel for the masses who did not have motor cars and kick-started the whole skiing revolution in the second half of the 20th century.

Road access in those early days was always a problem. Mountain road snow clearing had a low priority and high level roads like the A93 from Blairgowrie to Braemar were left uncleared for weeks at a time. The Cockbridge road from Corgarff to Tomintoul was frequently blocked for months at a time It was the first road in Britain to become blocked and the last to be opened. Even the A9 from Perth to Inverness could be blocked at

A snow plough, cutter/blower circa 1935. Still in use in 1952. Note the ancient chain driven cutter and primitive snow blower. A museum piece!

the Drumochter Pass which affected access to Aviemore and Cairngorm. That all changed in the early 1960s when both commercial and non-profit making chairlift companies opened up.

The winter tourist industry grew across the whole country, employment came to unemployment black spots and tens of thousands of people, most of them young people, discovered the challenge and the joys of mountain sport. Specialist sports shops opened in all the major centres of population and in towns on the periphery of the skiing areas. Bus companies, hotels, pubs, shops and business in general, benefited to some degree. Ski sport was a popular movement in Scotland and a revolution if you like, and it has been of huge importance to generations of young people in particular. As a commentator and writer about the sport, I have said it before and I shall say it again, we should never forget the social impact and the benefits ski sport brought to Scotland.

A Brief History

Glencoe has been described as the birth place of the modern skiing movement. In 1956 the senior club, the Scottish, invested in the first fixed ski tow on Meall a' Buiridh at the top of that dramatic glen. But Glencoe was also the home of a unique group of men from Glasgow who made a huge impact on the early development of the skiing revolution. They were originally climbers and only later skiers, who became ski tow and chairlift builders and became among the first ski instructors in Scotland. The late Frith Finlayson, was one such man and in his autobiography, "The Ski Teacher" he sketched out the great contribution made by his colleagues from the West of Scotland.

Much of the early history of the sport in Scotland was written from the point of view of the Scottish Ski Club with its membership based largely in the central belt and its history going back over one hundred years. The club

Ex War Dept surplus skis, boots and ash sticks circa 1952

has a vast archive and Myrtle Simpson, a past president of the club, dipped into that for her own book, "Skisters" published in 1982. Myrtle was the first woman to ski across the Greenland ice cap and is the author of many expedition travel books and children's stories. The emphasis naturally focussed on the fascinating historical background of the senior club and its important place through the last century.

This book offers a second view of what took place in the last sixty years and it is from a different perspective. The movement, the Golden Years of Skiing, involved so many people, some great characters and many achievements. Above all, it brought new challenges to new generations of young folk who suddenly became aware of the winter mountains. It comes from my own recollections with perhaps a different slant on events. For my generation, in the 1940s, the Eastern Cairngorms were easily accessible from Aberdeen and it was hill walking and climbing which were the first

Be warned! Skiing is addictive 22 snow flakes, 23, 24, 25, 26

attractions. Then, slowly but surely, we took to winter climbing and the options that snow added to our lives.

My contribution seeks to be more inclusive perhaps, for I found myself in at the beginning of so many early events relating to the Scottish Skiing Revolution. It began slowly in the 1950s, then exploded into the 1960s, "The Golden Days" being in the 60s, 70s and 80s when skiing became accessible and affordable for the majority and tens of thousands took part. Standards improved quickly and the demand for competition mushroomed at every level and, within a decade, Scots began to dominate in senior and junior British competition.

Going back in time to the first half of the last century, skiing had been an elitist sport practiced mainly in the Alps and by the English, while in Scotland the Scottish Ski Club catered for the few who could travel to Scottish snow or to the Alps. The second half of the last century saw major ski developments being built to cater for up to 20,000 skiers each weekend in high season. I was indeed lucky to be there at that time, to take part, to be involved in founding my home club in Aberdeen and to help create the national governing body for the evolving sport. And, above all, to be here at this time to enjoy recalling those bits of history.

Chapter 2

Uplifting Dreams

Mechanisation

The hard work in getting to the top of any hill is followed by the joy and the exhilaration of the downhill ski running. It is so difficult to try to explain just what the special buzz is and even to suggest that there can be a degree of addiction in the sport. Even in the pre-war 1930s, the Scottish Ski Club made several attempts to design machines to make life easier. In the beginning those early attempts were based on "Heath Robinson's" ingenuity. After the war the technology improved and by the 1950s the excitement demanded great things of our engineers. Those early ski tows pulled endless ropes around pulleys while the skiers attempted to hang on to the wet and frozen ropes.

The Scottish Ski Club created the very first fixed and permanent ski tow in Glencoe in 1956; the Dundee Ski Club followed suit in 1958 in Glenshee and within three and four years the major developments opened up at Cairngorm by Aviemore and in Glenshee in the east. Much later two other ski centres opened up. The Lecht, on the Aberdeenshire boundary with Banffshire by the old military road, opened in 1977 and in 1989 the Nevis Range on Aonach Mor adjoining Britain's highest mountain, Ben Nevis, opened up with the first gondola lift in the country. It was the sporting revolution; a period of several decades when Scots took to the winter mountains in their tens and tens of thousand and discovered a whole new world of adventure.

It was a time of great excitement and wonderful achievements. Time however, has moved on and ski sport around the world has progressed and

The basic rope tow. 1958

radically changed. Foreign travel is commonplace and ski resorts with high speed uplift and almost guaranteed snow have developed around the world. Better equipment, new technology and smoothly groomed ski slopes make it possible for most people to become adequate skiers in just a few weeks. Looking back in time, it was very much more difficult in the 1950s!

Early Days

In 1929 when the Scottish Ski Club reformed after the First War, regional branches across Scotland were created and organised occasional meets, many in the Central Cairngorms became popular. The records show that Dalwhinnie and Drumochter were used because they were served by the Inverness train and the hills were close to the villages. Ben Lawers by Killin

Opening of Nevis Range gondola in 1989

was also a focus and members ploughed uphill to get the good runs. It was there that a club hut was built and experiments were carried out with a ski tow and a tracked vehicle. A Citroen Kegresse shooting brake half-track was borrowed in 1937 and tested out unsuccessfully.

After the war, petrol was tightly rationed and very scarce but by 1950 the club had purchased a Weasel, an ex-army full-tracked carrier which was used at Dalwhinnie and at Drumochter with great success according to the 123 fare paying passengers in the first season. Not according to the Club Treasurer however, who was thought to have fainted when the petrol costs were revealed at a committee meeting. On steep and difficult terrain the Weasel only did one mile to the gallon.

News of big new ski developments in the Alps trickled through to Scotland but travel to the continent was still not possible for most folk in the 1950s, partly because of currency restrictions imposed by Westminster. Britain, the winner in a terrible war, had been bankrupted and foreign currency was not easily available. Also, rail and ferry travel was slow and costly, while air travel was still a dream. It was at that time that the older ski clubs began to have increased memberships and they were also experimenting and building ski tows, small ski tows, at home in Scotland. To even contemplate travelling to the Alps was beyond the means of the large majority.

Uplift was the buzz word and we all dreamt of the possibilities. Small rope tows came and went and we wore out countless pairs of gloves trying to hang on to the wet ropes. And then came the serious uplift equipment. My first encounter with a proper fixed ski tow was in Glencoe in 1956 when the "Glasgow Boys" were helping to complete that very first T-bar tow, inspired by Philip Rankin and the Scottish Ski Club. Time moved on and in 1958 I was briefly a navvy on Meall Odhar for the Dundee Ski Club (of all people, and, I never did get the promised free tickets in return for my labour) at the building of their first major tow at Glenshee. The rivalry between the cities of Aberdeen and Dundee had existed for many years as they jockeyed for the position of third city in Scotland. The rivalry carried over between the two ski clubs. But more of that later

The Boffins

Bill Blackwood of the Scottish Ski Club was perhaps the most persistent of tow builders for he doggedly designed, built and tested a series of machines. The skiing historians talk of his "insanely dedicated" group of friends who risked life and limb to help him drag unwieldy and hideously heavy contraptions up steep mountains. Some worked and some did not. The first broke loose and roared downhill on its own to disappear into a peat bog. Later, Mk II appeared on the Fiacaill Ridge on Cairngorm but it was also a fiasco. Several more followed with mixed success but the one I used, and enjoyed, was in the upper Corrie na Ciste in1958/9 and it consisted of a three wheeled garden tractor which did the job, but not without considerable risk.

Being dragged into the top pulley wheel was a risk and from time to time, there was blood on the snow. It could happen to the unwary, the young and the old and anyone who was careless and wore a long scarf round their neck or, if they failed to notice when their sodden gloves inadvertently became tangled up. Sisal rope has a knack, when very wet and under tension, of twisting. If it twists and grabs the end of a loose scarf or if it twists around a glove or a sleeve, then, quite simply, one tended to go round an old bus wheel. Now, think about it! Remember the sad tale of Isadora Duncan!

The top pulley round which the endless rope was carried, was in fact the wheel drum of an old bus. This was anchored to half a dozen old inner tyres linked together, from yet another old bus and this was the ingenious bit. This huge elastic band took up tension on the main rope, which fluctuated according to how many skiers were on the rope at the time. It was ingenious and I was certainly impressed. Blackwood was a real pioneer and a few years after his death I wrote my own appreciation of him for a ski magazine.

The Ghost in Corrie na Ciste.

"Bill Blackwood was a skier who hankered to get to the top, without perspiring. So, he built a strange machine in his garage, from a small three wheeled tractor, bits of string, some odds and ends and a very long rope. His name is still mentioned with reverence in certain quarters, together with the names of some of his followers, Hylas Holbourn, Ken Booth, Dave Duncan, Steve Stevenson and Jimmy Reid, all from the Aberdeen Ski Club. Oh, and many others, from other pioneering clubs.

The ghost of Bill Blackwood still haunts the upper Corries of Cairngorm, occasionally howling in frustration at the non-stop clanking of new fangled machines and at the crowds never before seen. There is no place in the new order of things for his kind of genius. No Blackwood masterpieces (and there were several) languish in industrial museums and yet of all the inventions of mankind, his early ski tows were marvels of ingenuity"

The boffins were also at work in the Aberdeen Ski Club and it was Dr. Hylas Holbourn of Aberdeen University who designed the club's famous Ferguson tractor ski tow Mk 1. His squad cut and screwed and bolted, turned wood, cleaned engines, dismantled, altered, rebuilt, tested, started again, spliced ropes and lifted and carried. The result saw duty on many Scottish hills and despite ruining many pairs of leather gloves, gave pleasure to hundreds if not thousands. It first appeared at the Lecht, where it survived an initial immersion in a deep peat bog, to give sterling service. It later saw action at Abergeldie, in Butchart's Corrie on Cairnwell and then in upper Corrie na Ciste on Cairngorm. The story of the many club ski tows in Scotland deserves more historical research, for there were many.

There were mountain huts and shelters too, on Ben Lawers by Killin, Meall Garbh in Glen Lyon, on Carn an Tuirc by Braemar, on Ben Gulabin by the Spittal of Glenshee and on Meall a Bhuiridh in Glencoe. On Carn an Tuirc the early skiing grounds of the Aberdeen and Scottish Ski Clubs there are few remains of a shelter hut and an engine hut for they were ceremoniously dismantled and cremated at the suggestion of the Invercauld Estate many years ago. As for the little diesel engine, it is buried in a peat bog just below the summit. Will a "TimeTeam" in later centuries scratch their heads and try to work out how the hell it got there?

Bren Guns and Tractors

Jimmy Reid was a prime mover in building powerful ski tows for his club, the Aberdeen Ski Club. His greatest success in earlier years was to buy a brand new ex-army Bren gun carrier, still in its wooden crate, for the incredible price of £120. It was delivered by rail and a small group of excited members watched in awe as it was hoisted onto a lorry and driven off for surgery. Jimmy Reid cut off the armour plating to reduce weight and then he modified the beast to operate the most powerful mobile rope tow operating in Scotland.

The Canadian built Ford V eight cylinder petrol engine purred into action to drive a 300 metre, endless rope on the lower slopes of the Cairnwell Tiger Piste at Glenshee, pulling 25 skiers at a time. The down rope was slung on short pylons and when there were only competent skiers on the up-rope and no beginners about, the man in charge would throw the engine into third gear to pull its human load uphill fast, very fast, very fast indeed! Today, such "dangerous" actions would be totally forbidden by law, under that mountain of Health and Safety legislation. For the two seasons before the Glenshee Company opened its first chairlift on the Cairnwell the Bren gun carrier reigned supreme. The Aberdeen members were privileged and jealous of their own powerful monster. It was club members first in the queue and extra charges for non-members.

The older Ferguson tractor fitted with half-tracks did equal service in summer and winter. First, at the Lecht for winter 1958 then in summer 1958 when it was harnessed to drag building materials up into Butchart's Corrie to build the Aberdeen Ski Club shelter hut, which still sits in a sheltered hollow below the col between the Cairnwell Ridge and Carn Aosda. The old Fergie Tow was the first of its kind in the club for its

Aberdeen Club Bren Gun Carrier 1959 with Jimmy Reid.

predecessors, all small mobile engine units mounted on skids and manhandled uphill, were great in their time but the drive was always for bigger, better and faster. Jimmy Reid, the club ski tow convenor, was a hero who had many willing helpers in those early days of uphill towage.

Windsails and Parachutes

David Soutar, a worthy gentleman of Aberdeen Ski Club knew Ben a' Bhuird near Braemar perhaps best of all. His expeditions using parachutes and wind sails took him over vast areas of the high plateau and on to the Ben Avon summits. Somewhere in the attic I still have an 18 foot RAF supply drop parachute modified with two wooden handles gathering the nylon cords together and I too experienced wind-assisted ski cruises on the same summits.

Parachute Uplift on Ben a Bhuird.

Para skiing was great fun and for a few years one could see several of the brightly coloured canopies being deployed on windy days. Just once, I flew up to the top of the White Lady without stopping and without colliding with any downhill skiers. It was just possible to tack across the wind on occasions to take action to avoid descending skiers but one or two did fall however, trying to avoid me, but that was their fault! Mr Clyde, the Manager of the Chairlift Company, was reported as being not too well pleased with the antics of the parachute brigade. He said in strong language that two-way traffic was not allowed on his mountain and so we diplomatically changed venues before he imposed sanctions. One did not argue with Mr Clyde. Para-flying could be a hazardous game but by gum it was great fun. The Aberdeen Club actually ran a few uphill Para Ski races for the diehards.

To finish this look at the parachute as an aid to uplift in Scottish conditions, I recall the experience of Gustav Fischnaller, the head of a ski school based in Glenshee. He arrived in Scotland in the 1960s and I met him as he became the course setter for many of the club and national race events held there by the Aberdeen and Dundee ski clubs.

Gustav was an adventurer and he was the first to fly off the top of the Cairnwell summit on his hang glider. I had never seen such a contraption before and I scrambled to get my camera as he swooped to land on the lower slopes by the Glenshee Ski Centre, luckily avoiding the many wire cables slung from pylons. He also used a parachute on occasion and his nemesis came close when he flew up to the summit of Meal Aosda from the lower Butchart's Corrie in a full gale and, misjudging his speed, he flew twenty feet into the air over the boulders at the summit before he could collapse his chute. He crashed into the rocks and broke bones and suffered many lacerations and bruises as he landed heavily. He was indeed a sorry sight for weeks after and he was a salutary lesson for other "flyers". Parachute skiers wanted to ski uphill for the excitement and at least cost. This was why the fine art was pioneered by Aberdonians, reputed to be the "canniest" of all Scotsmen. It's a lie of course, put about by those folk in Dundee. Yes, more of that later.

Up she goes

The Lecht

The fourth ski centre to open in Scotland was the Lecht in 1977. The hills in the area, at their highest, are just 2500 ft; much less than any other hill considered suitable for development. The road access is from the north by Tomintoul and the south by Corgarff and Allargue on the infamous A939 road. Infamous for it was once known as the first mountain road in Britain to be snow blocked and the last to be opened in the spring. It is a high road with many steep sections and Z bends and the height at the road summit is 2050 ft.

At the time Sir John Forbes of Allargue whose estate took in the hills around the Lecht was Hon. Pres. of the Aberdeen Club. We had his permission to ski on his land and to run a ski tow, as did the Moray Ski Club and the Keith Outdoor Club. He was sympathetic towards skiers in general for both he and his family of four daughters were involved. The Lecht Ski Centre with Jim McIntosh at the management helm and Prof. Jim Petrie, Peter du Pon and Ken Winram, as partners, floated the company.

Special Topography

The Aberdeen Club used the Lecht area in the 1950s, long before development took place. It was a popular spot, easily accessible from Dinnet and with minimum climbing to get to the best slopes. It was there that Michel Bochatay, a Swiss instructor from Chambery took his first classes in Scotland. Michel was brought over by the proprietors of the Profeits Hotel

Jim Macintosh, Manager at the Lecht

in Dinnet. (now known as Loch Kinord Hotel), when Lewis Mackay, the owner, saw the possibilities for the future. The Aberdeen Ski Club adopted the hotel as a stopping place both on the way to the hills and on the way home and the presence of a ski instructor was always a plus! His first Scottish season was successful and in the next year he brought over two more instructors and Deeside became Swiss territory.

On Speyside, the Austrian Ski School was well established in Carrbridge while Grantown on Spey was known for its Norwegian Ski School operated by Elif Moen. Further south, in Badenoch, Rudi Proshasca had established his own school. Aviemore had Frith Finlayson's Ski School d'Ecosse and many other ski schools came and went as the fortunes of the sport waxed and waned. Ski shops also proliferated rapidly across Scotland as the sport blossomed.

Swiss Ski Instructor Michel Bochatay 1958

The Lecht in only its eighth year of operation opened up a new slope by building the Buzzard Tow, a 550m long tow with the big capacity of 1,200 skiers per hour. The café was trebled in size and 300 new spaces were created in the car park. At that time the Lecht had overtaken the White Corries Centre in Glencoe in terms of skier capacity but not challenging ski runs. Historically, Glencoe was always known as the "Glen of the Weeping" and ski runs in the 1950s were given suitable names, The Haggis Trap, Mug's

Aberdeen Ski Club at Lecht 1958

Alley, Thrombosis, The Wall and the Cliffhanger Chairlift. The Lecht on the other hand named the ski runs in ecological fashion, Buzzard, Osprey and so on. Shortly after building, the Buzzard slope was inspected by the FIS (Federation Internationale de Ski) based in Geneva, who registered or homologated the slope as having the minimum length and gradient required to qualify for use as a slalom course for national races. This resulted in competitors in slalom having their times recorded and entered into the British and international seeding system provided an existing seeded skier had set the standard.

Who would have thought that could happen at the Lecht? The slopes are all under 2500 feet altitude, the runs are not long by any standard and are all heather slopes with no gullies or black runs to be found but, the Lecht has other

Left to right: Jim Petrie and Peter du Pon, Directors of the Lecht Ski Centre; John Hynes, Scottish Team Manager and Eric Langmuir, Principal at Glenmore Lodge, at Lecht

attributes! It is not too far from the townships of Moray and Aberdeenshire and from Aviemore and, it can be open for business when Cairngorm and even Glenshee have to shut because of high winds or even snow shortage.

By some accident of topography snow can be deposited on the more sheltered side of the huge central Cairngorm mountain massifs. Snow fencing has been essential for creating snow holding areas on all the Scottish skiing mountains. Cleverly placed fencing allows ski runs to be linked together, to cover rough ground and rock on exposed and windswept shoulders.

The art of trapping snow had been used before, beside high moor land roads and by railways where snow was trapped to fall more conveniently behind the fencing. To build them on a mountainside was harder work. No helicopters were available in the early days, even to carry the fence posts, the miles of wire and the rolls of heavy, split sycamore staves. When building the first of the chairs and tows much of the heavy building materials, stone and pylons had to be man-handled over rough terrain, sometimes using tracked vehicles.

All the five ski centres developed fencing and many kilometres are maintained to make skiing possible for so many. Some non-skiers complained over the years, about snow fencing and slowly the complaints about skiing developments in general became a very nasty battle culminating in the fight over Lurcher's Gully. I never knew how to describe the campaigners who were so active. Perhaps conservationists, greens, 'nimby's, anti-everythings, or old grouches? I'm one of the latter so I am well qualified to judge! In my case I just happened to be on the other side of that fence!

The fences are not pretty things when seen up close but from any distance and of course when filled with snow they are barely visible. The total mountain area used by skiers and their contraptions amounts to a few square kilometres among the thousands in the total area of the Cairngorm National Park.

PRICE LIST 1979/80
(Price includes CAR PARKING & VAT)

Day Ticket:	ADULT	**£3.00**
	CHILD	**£1.50**
5 Day Ticket:	ADULT	**£12.00**
	CHILD	**£6.00**
Season Ticket	ADULT	**£30.00**
	CHILD	**£15.00**
Family Season Ticket		**£85.00**

SKI HIRE

Complete set	ADULT	**£3.50**
per day	CHILD	**£2.50**
Skis and Sticks/day		**£2.00**
Boots per day		**£2.00**
5 day period Set.		**£14.00**
Skis and Sticks		**£8.00**
Boots		**£8.00**

Ski Instruction
Class for 2 hr per day **£1.20** per person

Private Lessons 1-5 persons **£5**/hour

Package Price. Including lifts, ski hire, accommodation, evening meal available from Colquhonnie Hotel. **Tel. Strathdon 210**

Ski-ing Group prices available on request at 24 hours notice. **Mondays-Fridays only**

Tel. No. Corgarff 240

THE LECHT SKI CO. LTD.
STRATHDON ABERDEENSHIRE

The cost of skiing at the Lecht

Chapter 3

Folk on the Hill

The Builders

Many great characters emerged during those early days of Scottish ski sport and deserve to be noted in any attempt to sketch a history such as this. Some of those from the West of Scotland, Glencoe in particular, became legends in their own time. Bob Clyde, who became the engineer who designed and managed the Cairngorm Chairlift Company from 1961, was a larger than life man. He was one of the "Boys" from Glasgow who helped to build that very first T bar tow on Meall a Bhuiridh in Glencoe in 1956. It was financed by the Scottish Ski Club and inspired by Philip Rankin who later operated the centre as a private venture for many years.

But while that first "serious ski tow" was the Scottish Ski Club's initiative, the practical energies of the men in the Glencoe Ski Club helped create it. That club was in many ways unique. One could not join; one had to be proposed and seconded and voted on and membership was restricted to one hundred. A certain amount of hard graft was demanded and if any member fell short in allotted tasks, he could be excommunicated, de-listed or just fired. In the beginning the club was basically focused on training youngsters to ski and race and to many others it was seen to be a happy commune with just a hint of Red Clydesider. The club continues today with a small membership but with a huge place in the history of Scottish Skiing.

In the 1950s Bob Clyde moved from Glasgow to work in Inverness while still doing much of his skiing in Glencoe. With Cairngorm being closer to hand he was aware of the plans by the embryo Cairngorm Winter Sports

Development Board to push a road up into the mountain and then, hopefully, to build lifts and tows. With the help of many organisations and even my own £5 donation in the 1950s, the Board finally persuaded the Inverness Council to contribute towards building the ski road from Glenmore to the foot of Coire Cas with the promise of more money for uphill development from the HIDB [Highland and Islands Development Board].

Something more than a hiccup then struck the Cairngorm plans. Disaster struck in the summer of 1960 when the mountain was hit by flash flooding which swept away several sections of the new road. Culverts were blocked by debris swept downhill and there was serious erosion in places. Inverness Council was quick off the mark and had the road and bridges reinstated before winter set in.

Bob Clyde. Manager of the Cairngorm Company.

At this point there was an unusual amount of cooperation between many local government bodies, landowners, businesses and ordinary well wishers. Mr Robert Clyde was in post but his plans to have at least one tow or chairlift in action for winter 1960/61 were foiled firstly by contractual problems with engineering suppliers and then by the road damage over the summer building season. Mr Clyde with his mountaineering, skiing and engineering background was the obvious choice for that job and he and his team had the Cairngorm Ski Centre up and running for season 1961/62. As they say, the rest was happy history.

It has been said that the early infrastructure was "Glasgow Built" for many of the men he knew in his own climbing and skiing days went with him to the Spey Valley. They all came from the climbing fraternity and from clubs such as the Creag Dhu, the Lomonds and the Glencoe Boys. From that group emerged the Glencoe Ski Club and subsequently several became ski instructors, some became staff members at Glenmore Lodge, others worked

A good day on Cairngorm.

for the Chairlift Company. I recall Bob saying to me in the 1970s, *"I was a engineer from Glasgow who designed and built industrial moving machinery. When fate took me to Cairngorm, I was able to use my skills to build the early ski lifts on the mountain. However, I found coal was a damn sight easier to shift than people and coal never complained".*

He was referring of course to the fact that in the early days of his work on Cairngorm the technology was primitive and constrained by lack of money. Breakdowns happened, cables would come off pulley wheels because of high winds, or more usually because some idiots liked to swing out and try to "slalom" uphill on the ski tow. When people stand in a queue waiting for an engineer to climb a pylon and laboriously hoist a heavy cable back onto a pulley wheel, delays happen, tempers fray and criticisms were directed at management. It still happens very occasionally in the Alps, even with all their sophisticated machinery. In Scotland, in the early days, it just happened more frequently. Bob Clyde was a tough character who did not suffer fools gladly but he always took any complaints from the public seriously.

Tom Paul

Harry Mckay, assisant manager on Cairngorm and an early Scottish Ski Champion with his son young Harry.

We will never know if he quite realised the impact his work had in the overall history of "Skiing in Scotland", in Aviemore in particular and on a much wider section of society. With hindsight, despite his award of the MBE, his contribution did go strangely unacknowledged until his death in 1994. Bob Clyde helped to bring a group of these Glasgow climbers and skiers with him in 1960 and it would be invidious to try to list them all.

I did know many of these characters during my mountain and skiing experiences. Tom Paul followed Bob as General Manager of the Chairlift Company, Harry McKay, Willie Smith, Jack Thomson, all settled in the Spey Valley, some to work at Glenmore Lodge and some with Clyde in the Cairngorm Chairlift Company. But, as I say, Frith Finlayson knew them all and placed them on his list of "pioneers" in his book, "The Ski Teacher". Significantly, they could all be categorised as "Clydesiders.

The Glencoe Doss

In his autobiography, published in 1997, Frith Finlayson goes into greater detail about the amazing contribution these Glasgow men made in the 1950s and through to the 1980s. Returning from national service, many men found a new freedom in the mountains and as Glencoe was in their backyard that was where it all began. Many conscripts had been stationed in Germany as part of the occupying forces and had been given the chance to ski while in the military.

Frith, together with his climbing and later his skiing friends, climbed extensively in Glencoe using "The Doss" as their base. It was a timber and canvas bothy built after the style of a tinker's humpy, sited discreetly and close to the access road up to the White Corries development in Glencoe. Lying in a hollow and very inconspicuous it served for the early years as the base for the "Glasgow boys", climbers and skiers.

By all accounts it was a sophisticated bothy or shanty and it, and the many characters it sheltered, has already become part of the history and mythology of Glencoe. Just nearby was Blackrock Cottage, the base of the Scottish Ladies Mountaineering Club, and they had just obtained a long lease from the local laird, Major Fleming. The black roofed cottage is one of the most photographed sights in Glencoe with its western backdrop of Buachaille Etive Mor and other Glencoe giants. Other climbing groups also adopted the area to camp and there were skirmishes between the groups but after time they learned to live in some sort of harmony. The laird even smiled at this invasion of his land after some basic rules had been established.

Glencoe Ridges

At Easter 1956 Frith and his mates were on Meall a' Bhuiridh in Glencoe helping to erect the first ever T-bar tow in Scotland, funded by the Scottish Ski Club. Also in the glen were four climbers from Aberdeen and founder members of the Aberdeen Ski Club, formed only two months before. We were staying in the Youth Hostel at the foot of the glen and were intent on having a week's climbing. We had heard on the grapevine that the Scottish Ski Club was building "something" on Meall a Bhuiridh and so we had taken skis with us on the off chance.

We were climbers from Aberdeen but were eager converts to the new sport. There were signs of activity on the upper slopes of Meall a' Bhuiridh as we climbed. First, we saw a few tall metal tripods with pulley wheels slung from the apex with half a dozen men heaving a cable over the pulleys. Then at the top, perched just on the dramatic summit, there was the most bizarre sight. A machine, sitting on top of a mountain, at 1108 metres. It looked like a farm tractor wrapped in a tarpaulin. First thought was, "How on earth did they get it up there?"

Our climbing group had in our time seen the remains of several crashed, wartime aircraft near summits in the Cairngorms and it was easy to workout how they had got there. Knowing mountain weather well, we could understand how easy is was to become totally disorientated in white-outs and clouds. Even with today's sophisticated air navigational aids, accidents still happen and two U.S. fighter jets flew into a snow covered Ben Macdhui in March 2001 and the two "top gun" pilots were killed.

After the war the RAF recovery units began to remove most of the engines and metal work on the Cairngorms but in the small debris, we

The ASC Ferguson tractor

always found the sad evidence of those war time mountain tragedies. I still puzzles me how on earth the "Glencoe Boys" and Philip Rankin's squad managed to get that big machine to the very summit of the steep mountain. Subsequently, we in Aberdeen Ski Club did manhandle various engines up other hills … with great difficulty. We also fitted half-tracks to a Ferguson tractor and took it up several hills. Our Bren Gun Carrier, converted to be our best ski tow had the power to operate from the foot of a hill. Fortunately, for it turned out to be too heavy, even with it's heavy armour plating removed, for the caterpillar tracks to cope with steep and rough terrain.

On Meall a Bhuiridh that year we were invited to help the "workers" put tension on the cable and told that if we came back later that week, we might see the whole contraption working. We climbed all the Glencoe ridges that week and after helping to put the final tension on the cable we became among the very first skiers to get to the top of that mountain on skis without breaking sweat. Unknowingly, that would have been my first encounter with the Scottish Club and the "Glencoe Boys" and I was fortunate enough in later years to get to know many more through my association with the Glencoe Ski Club at various race meetings.

Frith was part of that history of Scottish skiing, together with his contemporaries. And in his own book, he also chronicled the background to the immediate post Second World War, his early climbing days and his fascination and dedication in perfecting his skiing technique. He became a professional ski teacher, first in Glencoe and then, taking a huge gamble he moved his family to Aviemore to set up his own ski school. A ski shop followed and Ski School d'Ecosse flourished as Aviemore grew and expanded to become a major tourist destination in both winter and summer.

Frith said it was not just a profession for him, it was a way of life, and he went through hard and difficult times to become the supreme professional. One of the first instructors he employed when he began teaching in Glencoe, was Johnny Angelo. Later, on Cairngorm I always admired his smooth and flowing technique, so frustrating to watch. I just could not keep my skis together like the professionals. If I did, I tended to fall over. I put it down to having the wrong genes … or something.

Ed Pirie

It was years later that Ed Pirie, a good friend in the Aberdeen Club and, a BASI grade one instructor, told me to stop trying to keep my skis together all the time, it was more important to keep them slightly apart if I felt more comfortable that way. Ed Pirie came up through the Aberdeen Club junior ranks, winning club titles on the way and after an engineering apprenticeship, he took his professional training in Aviemore, and worked for Frith in the Ski School d'Ecosse. More about Ed later.

The Master

Karl Fuchs arrived in Spey Valley in 1954 and his own story was just as intriguing. Karl had been a policeman and ski instructor in the village of Styria in his native Austria and had survived fighting on the Russian Front during Germany's war in the east. He was a talented athlete and was in the Austrian Ski Team training for the 1948 Winter Olympic Games when he suffered a serious leg injury which kept him in hospital for many months.

Later, he married Eileen, an English girl who was studying in Austria.

They planned to open a ski school but, Austria was not too stable politically at that time as Russia was still an occupying power, together with the Western Allies. The couple travelled, before committing to settle anywhere and it was then they visited Scotland when Karl first saw the Central Cairngorms from the Inverness train and realised the potential for development. They bought the Struan House Hotel in Carrbridge and started the Austrian Ski School. which rapidly grew in popularity. His first clients had to walk and climb to reach the high snow slopes on Cairngorm but with beginners he had to find lower and more sheltered slopes. One of the first lessons I had from Karl was by the road from Grantown on Spey to Tomintoul, on a heather slope, just 20 minutes climb from the road.

Later he took us onto Cairngorm and a shallow gully below the Corrie Cas and below where Jean's Hut was sited in the early days.. A small burn flowed down the slope and was bridged by the packed snow which we skied and where we could hear the water running beneath. A few years later, I was on the mountain when news of a terrible tragedy spread by word of mouth. A young child had fallen into the burn when a snow bridge collapsed and had been swept under the bridging snow and drowned. I recall the day and the very spot, whenever I visit that site on Cairngorm.

Karl Fuchs, the Master

Hans Kuwall

During the period between 1954 when his Austrian Ski School opened and 1960 when the first ski road was pushed up into the Cairngorms, Karl was active in the movement for development in the Spey Valley. It was a slow process and frustrating for Karl and those who saw the potential. One of the first things he did was to bring over a young ski instructor called Hans Kuwall from his own village in Austria. This young instructor soon integrated, taking an English wife on the staff of Karl's hotel and later setting up his own ski school in Carrbridge. Hans then became a Scottish team coach and manager and eventually the manager of the Edinburgh Hillend Centre which was the largest artificial slope in Europe. Hans was known to several generations of young racers both on Scottish snow and in the Alps. His son Peter Kuwall followed in his father's ski steps as an instructor and manager.

My first ever ski holiday was in the Struan House Hotel in Carrbridge, in January 1957. I had been skiing after a fashion for some years with a group of close friends, all having come up through the Scout Movement and climbing clubs together. We were among the founder members of the Aberdeen Club the year before and five of our group got together to travel to Carrbridge and the Austrian Ski School. The Struan House Hotel was bustling, with other novice skiers and we five were packed into a tiny family room. There was snow on the ground in the village and it was our first ever hotel holiday together. Our more normal habitats had been tents, bothies, youth hostels, floors, stables, sheds and other exotic locations.

Peter Fuchs, the son of the house, was but a toddler under everyone's feet. The years passed and I got to know Hans well, in one capacity or another, on and off the hill. Meanwhile, Struan House was a fun place to be in, filled as it was with young people all intent on learning to ski. Eilean and Karl were very hard working hosts for the hotel was packed and, after skiing and dinner, there was much singing in the bar. I wonder still, how many of that enthusiastic generation can still be seen on the snow. I attended a reunion in Aviemore in 1995, when Eileen Fuchs invited staff and customers from the "old days" to celebrate with her. It was a big gathering with many English and Scottish accents and several Australians were there, who had been on the hotel staff during their "travelling years".

All sorts

Cairngorm attracted all sorts of folk. There were those who would ski wearing the kilt, worn with or without trews, but always a highly dangerous habit particularly when falling on ice. Then we would have groups in outrageous gear, top hats and evening dress and even ball gowns and evening cloaks. They could only have been students. Then of course there would be the occasional exhibitionist. The best known by far was a local chap, known to be a ski instructor who went down in Cairngorm folklore when he was photographed skiing down the White Lady in the buff, completely naked, unclothed, in a state of nature and in his birthday suit, but he had on his ski boots and a fine hat. He was a fine skier and the postcards produced became best sellers in Aviemore and further afield for many years.

Student snowmen builders

The Famous Backside

Chapter 4

A National Body. 1963

London Interference

The larger and more active clubs in Scotland, although fiercely independent, were aware that too much power lay down in London and were beginning to consider the need for some sort of coordinating body within Scotland. In the minds of the new activists in clubs in the north, London was too remote, out of touch and unaware of what was happening north of the border. Lewis Drysdale, a solicitor in Crieff, was the then Chairman of the Scottish Ski Club and he was well aware of the political situation. He and others from the S.S.C, did have regular contact with the Ski Club of Great Britain, {SCGB} founded in 1904 and the likes of the Kandahar and Downhill Only clubs based in the Alps. It was then that Lewis realised that the skiing movement in Scotland would be better with a larger degree of independence.

Lewis was alerted to the fact that the London based Ski Club of Great Britain was moving to form a federation to coordinate all ski sport in the UK, including Scotland. This news was not greeted well by the Scottish clubs which by then were growing in number and in influence. It was then that Lewis called the inaugural meeting in the Balmoral Hotel in Edinburgh (was the North British Hotel) in on 12th December 1963 and invited all clubs to say their piece.

This move for one Scottish body to coordinate the sport, was first floated the year before, following the publication of a letter in the Scotsman newspaper by the then Secretary of Aberdeen Ski Club. He proposed that the Scottish Ski Club as the senior club, should convene such a meeting. Events in London increased the urgency and the Scottish Ski Club then called the meeting of clubs and by early 1964 the SNSC was up and running. It was a time for urgent action. The embryonic NSFGB, (National Ski Federation of Great Britain) came into being later in 1964.

From the club representatives present at the first Scottish meeting there were the inevitable questions asked. " what do we get for our money", was but one and perhaps the most loudly spoken was, "what possibility is there that this proposed Council would become just another sub-committee of the Scottish Ski Club?" Politics, in ski sport as in every other walk of life, is a national pastime, with both the Dundee Club in 1937 and the Aberdeen Club in 1956, rejecting overtures by the "Scottish" to become regional branches of that senior club.

Many clubs and individuals contributed in so many ways to the skiing revolution which took place over four decades in Scotland. Eventually, there were over 100 clubs in Scotland with 93 full members of the national body. They represented around 14,000 skiers and in addition to that number, the Scottish National Ski Council offered affiliate membership to universities and colleges, private schools, all the Armed Services, large private companies, public bodies and youth organisations. Over 24,000 skiers eventually became involved with the Scottish Council and it was able to negotiate discount prices for day tickets at Cairngorm, arrange individual and group insurance and, importantly, assisted education authorities to introduce pupils to the sport by enlisting teachers and youth organisers to take the Ski Leader certificates. These were heady days as clubs and organisations proliferated.

Guy Chilver-Stainer with Chris Brasher

The Secretary Guy

A vital move at the very beginning of the Ski Council in 1963/4 was the appointment of an organising secretary. He was Major Guy Chilver-Stainer, a retired professional soldier and a holder of the Military Cross. He also had a good knowledge of Alpine skiing, having raced in the Arlberg Kandahar races before the war and, he was already working in Glasgow as the editor of a national ski magazine. Guy was a good organiser, a competent secretary and he soon overcame any initial resistance to him being a "Sassenach" in a den of hardened Scottish skiers. He filled that difficult position for many years as SNSC grew from strength to strength.

Frith Finlayson described Guy as "a foxy, lovable, wee rascal" That from Frith, was very high praise indeed. Guy was a great organiser who helped weld committees together, defused awkward elements and produced accurate minutes which satisfied the majority. He had a tough time over the years, and he inevitably ruffled feathers but with hindsight, I don't think anyone else could have done that job, at that time. Scots are by nature political animals, and if you put a Glaswegian, an Edinburgher an Aberdonian ... and I should perhaps add a Dundonian, together, the outcome could only be discord ... except when faced by the "auld enemy".

Lewis Drysdale sadly died following a car accident in 1978 but his contribution to Scottish skiing during it's golden years was immeasurable. He was essentially a Scottish Ski Club man who moved on to be the catalyst in bringing all the ski clubs in Scotland together in 1963. From 1950 he was a power in the sport, first through his own club and latterly by laying the foundations of a sensible structure for the administration of the sport on Scotland.

A friend summed up the man when he said that "Lewis brought enthusiasm, common sense, kindness, and a puckish and ever present sense of humour coupled with a sharp firmness for the over presumptuous, but above all, an endearing modesty"

He and Hamish Liddell from Pitlochry represented Scottish interests in the corridors of power in London for many years and in the British clubs which were traditionally based in the Alps. Hamish became the Chairman and President of SNSC during a decade, attracting many sponsors and representing Scotland in London where a strong man was always needed. In my years with the Ski Council we were all lucky to have Jim Currie of the SSC, John Wright, Aberdeen S.C. and Lewis Grant of Grantown on Spey representing Scotland's interests at the British Federation in London.

In 1972, the then President of the Scottish Ski Club, George Stewart, reported a membership of over 2,000. Coming up through the ranks of the junior racers was his own son Alan Stewart, who became a British Olympic skier and squad manager. The Scotsman newspaper estimated in 1979 there were 80,000 active skiers in Scotland and on any high season weekend there could be 20,000 on the ski slopes. Not all skiers were club-able of course, but all those who wanted transport or the use of shelter huts and other benefits such as insurance or discounted lift tickets, or had children or who were competitive, found club membership essential.

Alan Stewart, Olympic competitor

Here he comes. Proud parents.

The demand for competition increased rapidly among all age groups. Good skiers who graduated through the ranks and wished to race were swamping club events. The Scottish ski club already had a trophy cupboard full of cups and plaques first presented in pre-war days, and the Glencoe, Dundee, Aberdeen and Highland clubs were also running junior and senior club events, club championships and, amassing silver ware. One early success of SNSC was in creating a comprehensive Scottish national racing circuit, involving the major clubs and for both seniors and juniors. Many came to realise that the Scottish circuits were so successful and were attracting so many athletes from right across Britain, that they could in fact have been labelled British Alpine Ski Championships.

Competition did have a negative side. Race courses often used the best available snow with permission of the chairlift companies, and the paying public could become unhappy from time to time. When the Scottish teams were officially training they were given priority on one or two tows and lifts. At already busy weekends, long queues made the public less than sympathetic about the squads of hot shots using the best pistes.

Today, in a new century, many ski clubs have disappeared and the remaining ones have shrunk dramatically in membership numbers. The emphasis is still on junior training but the need for bus transport and ski hire etc., has gone, for many now travel abroad to ski. The Scottish Ski Club is still the senior club and one of the few remaining active clubs for competition. The wheel has turned full circle!. Perhaps this attempt to record the events of the glory days of Scottish Skiing is timely, before all the living witnesses, move on to new pistes. (I thought that was an elegant and sentimental way to end the chapter!)

Five Bob Fee

The resistance of a few clubs to join the new ski council in 1964 was because it was thought the five shilling levy on all members in the clubs was too much, bearing in mind that some new clubs were operating on a £1 annual subscription. The canny Aberdonians actually ran their club for the first three years, on the original subscription of just five bob, just to prove a point to the local branch of the Scottish Ski Club which had said that we could never run a ski club on a five bob subscription.

Bearsden eventually did join but earlier it was focusing on building an impressive club house and ski slope. Later when they had joined and had seats on the SNSC executive committee, they turned their publicity machine on, to criticise the Cairngorm Chairlift Company. In the Scotsman of 16th. January 1967 one half page was given over to, "An enormous list of grievances", a long letter to the Editor" signed by the shakers and movers of the Bearsden Ski Club. Namely: Chris Carter, Richard Butler, Craig McMillan, Douglas Brock, Allan Lindsay, and William Lockhart.

The complaints were principally about congestion and lack of lifts and tows on the mountain. This was just six years after the Cairngorm Chairlift Company began operating and the numbers of skiers had grown exponentially, swamping existing facilities. Robert Clyde, the General Manager and Engineer in charge was given equal space on the page and he gave convincing answers to the criticisms, with his plans for expansion in the pipeline. But, as we all found out later, there were other folk out there who wanted to throw spanners into the works of ski sport and restricted many attempts to provide more facilities for the young skiers.

West Coast Skiers

Bearsden was a thrusting club and today, it is the largest ski club in Scotland, with around 1,700 members and with a large social element … and licensed premises. As the numbers in ski sport grew, the clubs grew more professional and adventurous. Glasgow as a city was also switched on to the skiing boom and by 1967 seventeen new clubs had amalgamated to form the Glasgow and District Ski Clubs Association with over 2500 members It rapidly began to flex its muscles, first by shunning membership of the Scottish Ski Council. Several of these clubs disappeared by the end of the century as described earlier, as the need for club transport declined and the Alps became more attractive and available.

Glasgow and District Ski Clubs Association 1967

Anniesland College	Babcock and Wilcox
Bearsden	British and Norwegian
Central	Civil Service
Clarkston	Clydebank
Drumchapel	The Glasgow Club
Glasgow University	Greenock
Helensburgh	
Paisley and District	West of Scotland
Whitecraigs	

Glasgow Threat

There was discord in the west and in February 1970 the Glasgow Evening Times carried the headline, "Breakaway by clubs threatens Scots skiing". The article spoke of the threat to the Scottish sport if advanced plans to form an association independent of the Scottish National Ski Council went ahead. The rejection was largely because the five shilling annual fee [25p] per head required by the Council was thought to be excessive. The association was not new but had become an unofficial, unconstituted organisation, unrecognised by the Ski Council. The Evening Times balanced the arguments by pointing out the many benefits brought about by the Council, including the amendments to the new Transport Act which hugely benefited all ski clubs. It also referred to the road improvements made following representation to government and councils, lift tickets discounts and group insurance, etc.

Many clubs in Glasgow district have gone out of business but today the Glasgow Ski and Snowboard Centre has three slopes to cater for beginners and advanced skiers and a quarter pipe for snow boarders, in addition to a club house and a huge membership. Today, the national body for the sport, now called Snowsport Scotland based at the Gyle in Edinburgh continues to be the national body overseeing all aspects of today's snowsport ... group travel, insurance, racing and training from Bairns and Junior to British Teams, plastic slope coaching and snow instruction. So it can be said that Snowsport Scotland, the fledgling of the original SNSC, is alive and kicking. It all began in 1963, and it has moved with the times and matured.

Ski Council Officers. Circa 1975 Jim Currie, Mary Allison, Hamish Liddell, Kay Imray and Sandy Leven

"It's Scotland's Snow"

The Bearsden Club was anti-establishment in it's early days as was the Glasgow Association and they displayed their dislike or at least suspicion, of any "authority" or establishment bodies. They looked at the Aberdeen Club with suspicion as it had been a founding club in the Ski Council in 1963. I found that so ironic, for in founding the Aberdeen Club in 1956, my own group felt exactly the same about "authority" in any shape or form, hence the reason we started an independent club and refused the Scottish Club overtures. In founding the Scottish National Ski Council, we all felt we wanted to take charge of our own destiny, before the "London Establishment" could interfere.

Bearsden Club did eventually join SNSC, but it became a "difficult" club which always agitated … to begin with. However, they did make the skiing fraternity at large, laugh loudly when thousands of car stickers appeared around the country stating in bold print.

"It's Scotland's Snow"

No one admitted to the national prank but we had a pretty good idea that it originated in Bearsden. The slogan arose because of the congestion at ski centres particularly at weekends. It might have been an anti-English thing but more likely it was aimed at anyone viewed as "foreign" and who cluttered up the ski slopes and swelled the queues.

Ski Party Leaders

In 1968 the SNSC introduced the Ski Party Leaders qualifications which within two years became a nationally accepted certificate for teachers in Local Education Authorities and Youth Organisations throughout the UK. In the first year over 100 teachers and youth leaders were registered and, the British Association of Ski Instructors approved the qualification which replaced the BASI Grade 1V Ski Instructor which was discontinued by the hierarchy of ski instructors. Frith Finlayson, in his book, was scathing of the SPL scheme for he thought we, the SNSC, was encroaching on BASI territory. Frith continued to be critical even of his own organisation as it developed, by thinking that it was allowing standards to drop and too many instructors were achieving BASI Grade1. With so many strong minded characters involved in ski sport, it was inevitable that strife followed.

When the standards of BASI instruction in Britain had been established and accepted internationally the French saw serious competition from English speaking instructors and created all sorts of obstacles on the employment of British qualified instructors working in France. That long running conflict created difficulties for twenty more years until the "punters", the paying clients, made it clear that they wanted good English speaking instructors to teach them rather than the limited language spoken by so many French ski teachers. The ESF [Ecole de Ski Francais] fought a rearguard battle to defend their own territory and in places today, still do. BASI however grew rapidly to become internationally renowned with its 5000 members spread across the world.

Meanwhile in Britain the Scottish Council of Physical Recreation accepted the SPL [Ski Party Leader] qualification in their programme at Glenmore Lodge and other courses became available through the Compass Ski Centre, Glenshee, Perth and Kinross and Aberdeen County Community Services. Many other education authorities followed and a unified standard was then accepted with full support of the National Ski Federation of Great Britain. In many cases youth workers and teachers went on to take the professional qualification offered by BASI, both in the courses held in Scotland and on the Continent.

The SPL certificate allowed youth leaders to take groups into the mountains and to do so they had to demonstrate a basic knowledge of the sport, an all round skiing ability to an agreed standard and the ability to lead young people. BASI instructors of at least Grade III, then tested candidates in skiing ability.

As a result of this scheme thousands of young people in Britain were introduced to the sport. I would hazard a guess that many of those early pupils, who are now golden oldies, have passed on their love of ski sport to their own children and grandchildren who today, swell the numbers of Britons who head for the Alps every winter. They had first been given a taste for the sport by school teachers and leaders of the many youth organisations who were trained under the SNSC Ski Leader training scheme.

Chapter 5

The Old Club Bus

Before Private Cars

Many ski clubs were formed in the beginning, simply to provide affordable travel and, out of that came the social and competition element. The ski club bus was a great way to meet and make friends. There was much singing and fun on the way home after a day on the hills, as it always was, and is, among the walking and climbing fraternity. Guitars, harmonicas and lusty voices swelled the noise. Sadly, the ski bus is no more, or at least it has become a rare beast. The private car is the vehicle of choice today with little social intercourse possible while buses have now become huge, luxurious streamlined coaches with, piped music, television screens and thick piled carpeting … not at all suitable for muddy ski boots.

The early bus expeditions took us only as far as the bus could go. Sometimes that could be just to Braemar where the other roads were snow blocked. We would ski on sloping fields just outside the village or better still

on the good slopes at Abergeldie near Balmoral. Many times the buses could only go to the Shean Spittal Bridge just two miles short of the big hills at the Cairnwell summit. From there we climbed Carn an Tuirc where we installed a tow and a shelter hut. Sometimes we stuck and shovelled and pushed the buses out of drifts and ditches.

When talking about the "ski buses" in the 1950s and through until the 1990s, I would hazard a guess that there are thousands of Scots of a "certain age" still around, who will recall their own experiences of ski bus travel in Scotland. These coaches picked up and delivered home, the young, the not so young, the climbing converts and families with children, after a day on the hills. There was a lot of singing on board and more often than not, a "comfort" stop or two.

My own experiences with the Aberdeen Club when I served as the Bus Convenor would be pretty typical of what was happening all over Scotland. It was a revolution in mountain sport which had a significant spin-off for the many hotels which traditionally had a lean time in the winter months when they had to pay off staff and even close down in winter. When skiing brought Saturday and Sundays coaches filled with skiers on the way to or from the mountains, these hostelries, pubs and hotels were happy to open their doors. A number of hotels also began to have longer stay guests during the winter weeks as the ski tourist trade built up. Highland villages and towns soon felt the benefits of the rush to the winter mountains. Significantly, by 1972 the percentage of unemployed in the Spey Valley was just 2% while the national average was 7%.

The opening of the Aviemore Centre in 1966 was a main focus in the Spey Valley but before it opened, Grantown on Spey, Nethy Bridge, Carrbridge, Boat of Garten, Kingussie and Newtonmore were enjoying the new business. Eventually, when the centre did open they suffered from the competition.

When the Lecht opened in 1977, Tomintoul and even Corgarff gained from winter travellers while on Deeside, Braemar flourished and, Ballater to a smaller extent. Weekend passing trade benefited many hotels up and down Deeside. I can think of at least ten where weary skiers sought sustenance of one sort or another, on a regular basis. On the south side of the Devil's Elbow, Dundee territory, bed and breakfast houses became busy and some built extensions to cope. The Spittal of Glenshee Hotel, rebuilt in 1960 after a major fire, was hugely popular for many years and the Dalmunzie Hotel tucked up under Ben Gulabin had been a favourite place for Dundee skiers even before the war, and Blairgowrie got a large share of the new business. Whenever major race events were held at Glenshee, Dalmunzie became the Race HQ for Dundee officials and sponsors.

Comfort Stops

When Profeits Hotel in Dinnet, half way between Aberdeen and Glenshee and a regular stop, had two coaches arriving on the way home on a winter evening, it could cope with the rush. When three coaches arrived they were stretched to the limits of space even when given prior warning. When four or more coaches arrived, only larger hotels could cope, and they invariably made big efforts to do so. Business was business. Club bus convenors had to run a tight service to satisfy all their members. Many were young folk, a few under drinking age. Some were families with kids eager to get to bed early. Road travel in those early years took longer, faster vehicles and straighter roads allow faster travel today.

Most called for a comfort stop, something to eat, a pint or a hot toddy and on big nights as at prize givings or racing victory over Dundee, a dance or two. All needs were catered for, most of the time, but convenors had to be tough to be fair to the majority. The boys in the back seats invariably heckled the bus managers when the whistles went for the coaches to head home. It was not unheard of, for a bus to depart home with one or two recalcitrants left standing, to find their own way back to Aberdeen. Once, just once, one member was abandoned in Aviemore for being late, too late. Herbie by name, he later became a stalwart committee man for many years and who, ironically became the Bus Convenor who ruled with an iron fist.

The Fife Arms in Braemar, the Huntly Arms in Aboyne, the Burnett Arms in Banchory were among the hotels prepared to cope with these big weekend invasions. With perhaps two to three hundred, damp, thirsty and hungry skiers all to be fed and watered in under one hour, it was some feat. But they were alerted well in advance to cater for us. Occasionally, an extra bus load from another club would pull up unannounced, having spotted where the "action" was.

On special occasions like club race days and prize givings, the hotels would bring in a couple of musicians and no time was wasted getting on to the floor. The sound of a couple of hundred skiers "heuchin" in unison was awesome. From the hoteliers point of view their entire staff had to be on alert for the arrival of the ski buses. The doors would burst open and in would rush the mob. First to reach the bar would relay the order, "Ninety three plates of stovies please and forty pints of beer, seventeen drams and a hundred and twenty one packets of crisps".

Oh My Lord

Some villagers might have thought all these "goings on", on the Sabbath were inappropriate. One minister of a Kirk in the centre of Aberdeen, took the initiative to redress the balance. His church in the city centre was beside the 8am pick up point every Sunday morning when coaches would load up. He liased with the club and arranged to open his church and hold brief Sunday services at the same time. The ski bus rules were normally adhered to, "If you are not at the pickup point when the bus is due to go, THE BUS WILL NOT WAIT". That winter, the time-table was slightly modified, and the church service was radically shortened. And so, all needs were catered for!

Shortly after opening in 1963, it was announced that Mar Lodge was to open the Estate Chapel on Sundays to accommodate skiers. Sadly, that never happened for the Mar Lodge dream was just that, a dream.

Ski bus services were running all over the country and the Aberdeen. experience was typical of many clubs. One ski shop in the city centre volunteered to take bus bookings from members popping into the shop or telephoning. The bus convenor picked up the lists at close of business on Thursdays and called the coach company to confirm numbers. Sub-contracting

ASC Ski Bus Crowd 1964

by coach companies became necessary as perhaps half a dozen coaches were required for the Aberdeen club alone and then there was the University Club and the Aberdeen Branch of the Scottish Club, the Post Office Club and climbing clubs and so on. Without any available statistics, it was apparent that many scores of coaches headed to the hills at weekends, from the cities, towns and villages of Scotland. Clubs sprang into being in the Borders, in Carlisle and Newcastle and they were prepared to make long trips for only one day on the snow. On many occasions I referred to the "Ski Fever" gripping the country.

The London/Cairngorm Express

For several seasons, the London Weekend Ski Club coaches left that big city at the end of business on a Friday, to drive overnight to Newtonmore in Invernesshire, arriving at 7.30 am. There the skiers breakfasted, changed into ski gear and were on Cairngorm as the lifts and tows opened. Returning to the hotel in the evening, they no doubt enjoyed Highland hospitality before catching up with their sleep. On Sunday they had a full day skiing before dining and changing in their hotel, to drive overnight back to London. This

Full car parks at Glenshee

continued for several seasons with two or three coaches each weekend making the long journey, particularly when Scottish snow conditions were at their best in mid season.

The bus park at Cairngorm could be congested at peak season and coaches had to disgorge the passengers and return to Glenmore or Aviemore to park. Later, a regular bus service ran from the Spey Valley to Cairngorm, to cater for the local resident skiers and for drivers unable get into the mountain car parks. Congestion either in car parks or tow queues was always a problem. But at least the chairlift queues were orderly, unlike France where chaos and blatant Q jumping were rife and can still be. The penalty for Q jumping at Cairngorm was severe.

Similar congestion was happening at Glenshee where the police sometimes had to turn away cars and coaches which were forced to disgorge their passengers and continue to Braemar to park up. Soon the local authorities undertook massive extensions to the Glenshee car parks, with room for 1000 cars and vans and 70 coaches. Which brings to mind again, the early rivalry between the Dundee and Aberdeen clubs. In 1960 when both clubs were operating club ski tows in the area, the new Glenshee Chairlift Company began operations to build their first commercial chairlift. For some reason the company, floated by leading members of the Dundee Club, chose the only bit of flat ground by the roadside where Aberdeen had, by tradition, been parking their coaches. While the north skiers flocked to use the chair lift, they also had to dig out another piece of ground to park their buses. The muttering did not last long because uplift was far more important than a muddy old bus park. Thankfully, Grampian Regional Council rushed to extend car and bus parks. Once upon a time one could count 70 ski buses in the Glenshee parks and hundreds of cars.

Not Guilty

The timetable for the Aberdeen club bus services was widely known and of necessity, strictly adhered to. It began at the bus depot in the north of the city and picked up at ten points as it proceeded through town and out onto the North Deeside road. Or, if Lecht was the destination, it headed towards Alford. For Cairngorm the buses went by Inverurie. There were pre-arranged pick-up points en route. The system was honed over the years and by the 1970s and 80's when the membership was around one thousand, it really was a huge logistical operation.

The call for Saturday transport grew and when skiing conditions were at their best, Aberdeen was moving 700 people over two days at the weekends. Failing to book in advance could result in being turned away as the buses were invariably full and no standing was allowed. The sleepy heads who booked but failed to turn up, were given one warning and a system of fines operated thereafter.

In 1960 the bus convenor was visited by local police detectives investigating a serious incident in the city. They wanted to check the lists of skiers actually present on the ski buses that weekend. Now, I can confirm that it was eventually proved that the accused was not a member of the Aberdeen Ski Club, nor was he a skier. I shudder to think what headlines the Dundee Ski Club would have made, if in fact we had harboured a villain. Our clubs were bitter rivals. But more of that later.

At the start and end of the season when numbers travelling might be low, cooperation with other clubs did happen, if the Scottish or Aberdeen University ski club coaches were only partly full it was to everyone's advantage to share. Rivalry persisted of course. Aberdeen City Council Transport Department realised that there was a demand for public transport to Glenshee and started up in opposition but they were late on the scene. The need for coach travel was slowly on the wane as more private cars came onto the roads. The Aberdeen Corporation bus service did function, but only for a brief period. People had more money and free time and most importantly, flights from Scotland to Alpine destinations were just becoming available. The lure of guaranteed snow and better weather in Austria, France, Italy, and Spain and then the East European countries was strong and slowly but surely, cheaper and more frequent flights became available. Supply and demand!

Up, Up And Away

There were problems for those who were able to contemplate flying to the Alps. The frustration was the doubling of flight costs and travelling time, merely to get to London which was for a while the only jumping off point for any Alpine destination. The Ski Council took the initiative in 1968 by advertising in its Scotski News which all club members received, that one airline had agreed to open flights direct from Glasgow to Geneva. This seriously cut the costs and the time for Scots to get to the Alps. It also boosted membership of affiliated clubs.

Despite the plunging value of sterling, many still wanted to ski abroad and later the Bearsden Ski Club with its flair for business, stepped into the travel business and their target was the general skiers market, not just for their club members. It was a big step and it succeeded. Expo Flaine was a serious excursion into the complex holiday market and they contracted with the new French ski resort for 5,000 bed nights, which amounted to 25% of Flaine's entire British market in a season.

The package used luxury coach travel between Scotland and the French Alps, involving approximately 23 hours overnight travel with a ferry journey. The coaches were state of the art with a television screen, reclining seats, a toilet and a cocktail bar ... well, a couple of crates of beer. These ski club entrepreneurs knew the business they were in, for they sent one of the new Parks of Hamilton Coaches around Scotland on a promotional tour. I was seduced by the comfort of those ultra modern buses having spent my very early skiing and climbing days, travelling in old, well worn, no frills, economy class vehicles, one even was a pre-war charabanc. I chose one, three day Bearsden Club trip to Flaine together with two of my children and it proved to be, what shall I say, unusual and eventful. The drive south from Glasgow was fine until we reached middle England, where sudden minor snow falls seemed to cause road chaos. We reached that area in the middle of the night.

Nightmare

One section of a minor motorway was closed off just as we reached it and the coach was redirected towards ... goodness knows where in the English hinterland but, the Bearsden Courier knew better. The roads official, obviously did not appear to know what the larger picture in his region was and so, when he left, we removed the diversion sign and continued on our intended way. We replaced the "closed road" sign of course. There was only a couple of inches of snow on the road and because it was closed to other traffic we made good time for another 70 miles and all the way down to Dover and the cross channel ferry.

We then encountered real snow in France as we approached the Alps but, had few hold ups until the last 10 kilometres to Flaine. Even with chains, our coach slithered gently off the road and stuck fast near a French Army Mountain Troop barracks, just two kilometres from our resort. The 23 hour trip became a 28 hour nightmare where we ended having to carry our luggage and skis the final 2 kilometres to find our hotel, in the dark and in a snow storm. My kids found it all a bit of an adventure but they were young and their Dad just needed his bed!

Chapter 6

Dundee V Aberdeen

City Rivalry

A simmering battle had long been waged between the cities of Dundee and Aberdeen. For a century or more, each jockeyed to be known as the third city in Scotland on a population basis. Dundee had Jute and prospered. Aberdeen had Fish and Granite and prospered. It was when Aberdeen acquired an Oil Industry in 1974, its population and its prosperity grew and grew, leaving Dundee in fourth place. A jocular battle also festered on between the two Ski Clubs from the beginning and still do in the dark recesses of old memories. Dundee undoubtedly had the best ski race team … in the beginning, but Aberdeen

Helen Jamieson, Dundee Ski Club and Olympic skier with Sir John Hunt.

overtook them in the end. Both racing clubs produced Olympic team members.

When Dundee Ski Club was in it's hey-day in the late 1950s it took a bold step and went ahead to build a fixed T-bar tow on Meall Odhar, the first of it's kind in Glenshee/Glen Clunie. That summer, the Aberdeen Club people were working in Butchart's Corrie in the shadow of the Cairnwell and to the west of Meall Odhar, where we built a substantial shelter hut, which still stands today. We offered to help Dundee and were invited to do some mountain navvying. The rewards were to be one day's free ski ticket for each day labouring. Came winter and on the opening of the tow the deal was forgotten but we didn't make a fuss. Well, not at the time. It was when the commercial Glenshee Ski Centre opened in 1962 when the Aberdeen skiers became irritated. The two Honorary Editors of these clubs were responsible for fanning the flames but now, they are both too old to bother. Well, perhaps I may be allowed to fire a final shot. From the very start in 1962 when the Glenshee Chairlift Company opened for business, many folk in Grampian Region objected to that off shoot of Dundee Ski Club, calling itself the "Glenshee" Company. All the splendid facilities, lifts, cafes, first aid suite, toilets, ski hire unit, ski school and ski slopes were, and still are, actually in Glen Clunie. It was David Jamieson, a founder of the Dundee Ski Club in 1937 and his cohorts, who financed and built that welcome ski centre … in Aberdeenshire. The entire ski area is patently in Glen Clunie and every ordinance map confirms the fact.

Geographically Wrong

In fact, Glenshee is nowhere near the boundry between Perth and Kinross and Grampian Region. The boundary is between Glen Clunie and Gleann Beag while the real Glenshee lies several miles to the South, below Ben Gulabin and by the Shee Water. By the way, the translation of Glenshee from the Gaelic, is, "Glen of the Fairies".

But I wasn't the only one to object! I dug out a letter I received in 1969 from Marcus Humphrey, the Laird of the Dinnet and Kinord

Estates adjoining Balmoral Estate, in his capacity as Chairman of the Deeside Tourist Association. We had been discussing the recently published report by Aberdeen University entitled Royal Grampian Country, and he also had a bee in his bonnet about the miss-naming of the Glenshee skiing facility.

He pointed out that his organisation had been fighting the anomaly from the beginning because it had been detrimental to tourist business in Aberdeenshire. He had persuaded his County Council to erect road signs at various points to inform people that they were entering "Royal Deeside". He had also received an assurance from the Ordinance Survey that they would correct their mistake in naming the hill at map reference OS 135774," Glenshee" instead of "Cairnwell". Yes! Dundee was in the dog house again.

The Centre

Technically Wrong

Forty years later the problems still grumble on. Peace had more or less been created between the two ski clubs but the politicians were hard at it again. In the new century, a further attempt was made by Perth and Kinross to have the Boundary Commissioners move the "Glenshee Ski Centre" into their district. Their case was that they had the upkeep of one half of the access road to the centre but none of the benefits from rating and community charges which go to Grampian Region. It could be a problem for all concerned for many more years. So, don't hold your breath.

A typical illustration of the rivalry between the third and fourth cities of Scotland is found in the following letter from the Hon. Editor of D.S.C annual magazine to his Aberdeen counterpart

Robert J. Benzies,
Couper Angus
Perthshire

To The Editor, A.S.C. Journal 1966

Dear Ed
You wrote me away back in May and even gave me your phone number, with the suggestion I write a piece for your Journal. Firstly, I lost your letter but then you rang me and said I could be as rude as I wished about you all. Then I was immediately interested. Thank you for a copy of your publication and I apologise for the further delay. I have been busy writing to all your advertisers to see if I can get them into the Dundee Journal. That's the kind of people we are, as all your readers probably know.

I still don't know why I should write a piece, when I have my own Journal to fill, and, from the top bunk of the psycho-analyst's couch, I still don't know what's wrong with Aberdonians. Individually most of you are okay ... take Peter Emslie; who is your greatest ambassador ... he bought me a pint just a year past February.

But lets face it … the only place where Aberdeen comes before Dundee, is in the dictionary and I have also been working out the logic of a comment I read in your last publication. The insinuation was that Dundee racers trained on beer and women. This could get you boys into a lot of trouble, because if our training methods are more successful, and if we accept that the national brews of beer are the same across the country, then your women can't be up to much … just a thought.

I hope your Journal, without an article from me, goes from strength to strength. Unfortunately, my committee have heard that you make it pay and are even making a profit. Now they are expecting me to do the same. My apologies once again for not sending you an article.

Yours aye,

Bob, Editor D.S.C. Journal

Bob and I worked together over the years on the Ski Council and on the hill. I should perhaps apologise to him, for in preparing this book, I use a couple of cartoons and one photograph taken from his 1972 Dundee Ski Club Annual Journal. It is said that plagiarism is the highest form of flattery!

Believed to be Dundee Ski Club Committee 1972. Further comment is unnecessary.

Glenshee Changes Hands

There were a series of less than good seasons at the end of the last century and the Jamieson family group, the original investors in the Glenshee Company in the early 1960s, called it a day. Glenshee, became home territory for the Dundee Ski Club in 1937 and David Jamieson was a leading light.. He became a driving force in the club and then in the development of the major commercial ski centre in the 1960s. His background was in the jute industry which saw Dundee prosper for over a 150 years and he brought a strong personality and a good commercial understanding to Scottish skiing. There were several good years when the seasons were long and the weather was kind.

There was no rush to take over the company, because snow shortages were creeping in and the business didn't look too good. But, a group, including some of the original ski centre staff were enthusiasts and took the gamble.

The Hub at the Cairnwell Cafe. Glenshee

I had always admired that group which bought over the Glenshee operation when the future of skiing was becoming uncertain. Like many other skiers we were delighted for them, in winter 2009/2010 when the big snows came, the car parks filled and even the sun shone. There were seven original staff members who took over the company in September 2004 and they were soon joined by ten local investors who also became "hands on" workers. They struggled from time to time but only one winter, 2006/7, was "seriously poor". As a form of insurance, the company had invested in six snow making machines which ensure that beginners slopes have enough snow.

Following the wonderful 2009/2010 winter, plans have already been passed to build a new chairlift from behind the main building, to the hub area at the foot of Butchart's Corrie. It will be a short chair but it will serve the five ski tows which fan out from the hub, where the hexagonal shaped Cairnwell café sits.

Chapter 7

The Anti Brigades

Discord

The hills of Scotland can be lonely and sometimes bleak and we tend to think of them as our wilderness, stark, romantic and beautiful. Traditionally they give pleasure and sport for those who shoot and fish and, work for those who manage the vast estates. Skiing came on the scene, slowly and quietly but when the rush opened in the 1960s, things changed. The new sport brought development and crowds to a few big mountains. There were those who objected and condemned the invasion but for many years it was an unstoppable movement.

1979 was a critical year for it saw the beginnings of an united front by the conservation lobbyists as they put more pressure on the politicians to stop further ski developments on Cairngorm. It also brought loud calls from Cairngorm Sports Development Ltd., the company running Scotland's principal ski area, to allow further developments to satisfy the still growing demands. Already by 1979 major international ski competitions had come to Cairngorm and to Edinburgh Hillend's Ski Centre with huge implications and recognition within international ski sport. This article summarised the situation that year.

Cairngorm Conflict   *The Scotsman* January 1979

Ed Rattray finds that ecology and development are on a collision course in the Spey Valley.

A major planning document covering the future development and conservation of the entire Cairngorm region, lies gathering dust in St Andrews House. The Cairngorm Area Report was published in 1967 by the Scottish Office and it was followed in 1969 by Royal Grampian Country, a detailed study of the resources and needs of the area prepared by Aberdeen University for the Scottish Tourist Office.

Both studies concluded that a policy of development within a scientifically organised system of conservation was the only way forward to improve the economy of the region, provide the demand for recreational space and yet retain the qualities of remoteness and tranquillity which are so important.

The subject has been highlighted by proposals put forward by Cairngorm Sports Development Ltd, the non-profit making company which runs Scotland's principal ski area. The plan to double the size and capacity of the ski area has the unqualified support of the skiing community as represented by the Scottish National Ski Council and the burgeoning tourist industry in Spey Valley. On the other hand there has been alarm expressed by the conservation lobby and opposition to further incursion into a wilderness area.

The problems of growing queues at all Scottish ski centres and despite increased capacity, the problem is still acute at peak periods. Speaking of the 10 year -plan, Miss Kay Imrie, Chairman and Vice President of the Ski Council speaking on behalf of 14,000 club skiers and indirectly, many tens of thousand more, said, "The proposals are modest and long overdue and are likely to be inadequate before the programme is completed.". The problem is, in the eyes of many, the responsibility of the planning authorities who have been quick to encourage the building of profitable tourist hotels in the Spey Valley while ignoring the imbalance in the ratio between tourist beds and uplift capacity at ski centres.

At a meeting of ski interests in Braemar, Mr T. Huxley, Assistant Director of the Countryside Commission in Scotland highlighted the problems that accrue when roads and lifts give uncontrolled access to ecological fragile areas of the Cairngorm plateau. The damage comes not from the thousands of skiers during the snow season but from the walkers and climbers who are given quick and easy access to the plateau and mountain tops by the ski road and chairlifts. Protect the Wilderness, is an emotive phrase and one which is perhaps out of context in

Scotland. In North America, true wilderness areas still exist where man has had no impact on the face of nature because of the vastness of scale. The Americans have come to terms with too many cars and too many people. Their National Park systems for 70 or more years, have been protecting the larger wilderness by channelling people into carefully selected and developed areas and restricting walkers to prepared tracks.

In Scotland, as in many regions in Europe, man has been responsible for much of today's landscape. Even our most remote and lonely mountains and glens have been sculpted by past generations. Felling and burning of indigenous timber together with old and new agricultural and sporting practices, have changed not only the appearance but also regional micro climates and this over as short a period in our history as 300 or 400 years. The heritage of mountain and glen must be carefully managed and protected against the increasing demands of modern society. And yet, the need for mountain recreation is legitimate and necessary in today's world. The answer must lie in the American experience of "Develop to Preserve", the diverting of people into prepared tourist and recreational regions thus protecting the remaining wild areas and this can only be achieved by good planning.

The ecologist would be the first to agree that all is not gloom and despondency, as a team of scientists from the Institute of Terrestrial Ecology at Banchory have shown.. In work published following a lengthy study on Cairngorm, Dr. Adam Watson and Dr. Neil Bayfield showed that the ptarmigan, that noisy defender of our highest mountains, has come to terms with progress. The study showed that far from being driven off by the presence of hundred of skiers, the birds continue to feed, breed and nest, in some cases within yards of the late spring and early summer snow patches.

Erosion is a major concern whenever development of any kind is undertaken. In contrast to the early works on Cairngorm, in the 1960s, much of the later works were sensitively achieved with the use of helicopters. The results were dramatic. Around the newer installations, vegetation was largely undisturbed and any damage was reinstated and earlier scars reseeded. It is hoped that by the end of this ski season, discussions will have taken place, differences resolved and firm plans laid to overcome the growing congestion at peak periods.

More exaggeration

Differences were not resolved and just six years later, the Scottish Wild Land Group and the North-east Mountain Trust were being accused of arrogance and exaggeration by people in high places. Why you may ask? For saying that Scotland was not suitable for downhill skiing. Thousands of Scots blinked in disbelief when they read these statements. (Cairngorm recorded 347,902 skier days in season 1986) And yet that was the continuing doctrine of those who condemned the very existence of skiing, a major sport and tourist industry. This was being said when the clamour for more ski facilities was at its loudest. The high priests of conservation were riding high on the crest of popular opinion which they were whipping up.

The final arrogance came when the activists constantly suggested that skiers were a race apart, *"litter louts, despoilers of the environment, who aid and abet greedy land developers and speculators"* There were major inconsistencies in the emotional arguments being used by some conservation spokesmen and regrettably there were too few, prepared to argue for consensus. Re-reading those news reports, I am not surprised that so many felt aggrieved at all those attacks on the sport which I and tens of thousands of Scots enjoyed so much. Why on earth did we allow their strident voices to block such a popular sporting movement. The Rambler's Association became very vocal and at an annual conference in Salford, two senior members were reported as saying, *"Walkers cause little environmental damage on mountains"*.

Tim Whittome the spokesman for Cairngorm Company, then pointed out that astonishingly inaccurate information which was spread about, was seldom rescinded. He cited one statement made by the Ramblers *"The ski area is managed as if it were nothing more than a dump for wrecked cars"*. Mr Betts at the Rambler's Conference then spoke of the dangers to the dotterels, but just demonstrated his ignorance.

Dr.Adam Watson had earlier studied the dotterels and reported that when they migrated from Africa to nest in early summer in the Scottish mountains they showed remarkable tolerance of disturbance, *"so long as nobody actually stood on them"*. Finally there was either a major typographical error or blatant and dishonest exaggeration. A Mr. Griffiths in the Rambler's, asserted that the new proposed ski area in Lurcher's would cater for 30,000 skiers. The published truth was that the figure was estimated at 1,000. The protagonists continued to tell their half truths, lies of omission and outright whoppers.

One private concern of mine was about the allegations made by the Ramblers, by talking about "a dump for wrecked cars" in the Cairngorm car parks, could they possibly have been talking about my old Morris Minor Traveller? If it was, then I was prepared to take serious umbrage! One had to laugh at some of the farcical statements being made by the "conservationists". But, it was not a laughing matter.

But there were a few more important voices being heard and one was the Chief Scientist with the Nature Conservancy Council (now Scottish Natural Heritage) when he resigned his post. Dr. George Black describe the actions of the NCC as *"uncompromising militancy"*. In his post he advised the council on land all over Britain which should be protected as Sites of Special Scientific Interest, (SSSIs). His concerns had been the swift move away from conservation by co-operation, to that of dictat. His final words were, *"I did not feel that I am professionally qualified to select SSSIs on cultural, recreational, inspirational or spiritual grounds"*. Sadly his voice was drowned by the overwhelming voices of the "anti brigades".

Even More Conflicting Evidence

Technically speaking, Scotland was a land of perpetual snow until weather patterns changed. Or very nearly! There had been but a handful of years in the whole of the last century when all snow completely disappeared from the high corries of the central Cairngorms or from the steep gullies of Ben Nevis. These rare occasions were recorded in climbing club annals and they were the subject of study by Dr. Adam Watson of the Institute of Terrestrial Ecology in Banchory. Long before he became an Ecologist and from the age of seven he accompanied his father to log these snow patches. By 1979 he had been measuring their size and location for over thirty years. Very often by late July and August the snow fields were reduced to patches of dirty grey snow lingering in the shadows of the northern facing corries. They were of no more than academic interest but, sufficient to allow us to boast of *"Scotland, land of river, mountain and everlasting snow".*

It was a close run thing in 1981 when we endured the poorest ski season for 16 years but while there was little snow for skiing in winter, fickle nature left snow patches on Ben MacDhui at around the 3,900ft.level throughout the year. There appeared at that time to be no snow lying in the dark recesses of Garbh Choire of Braeriach, the source of the River Dee. But, Dr. Adam's studies at that time seemed to supported the theory that the climate was actually getting a touch colder.

His sightings of an increased number of birds in the central Cairngorms, normally found in Sutherland was one pointer to what the more enthusiastic climatologists at that time claimed, was an approaching ice age.

While damage had been done during the early development of the ski facilities attempts to repair the scarring was carried out by the chairlift company. Following the re-seeding programme, Neil Bayfield also at the Banchory Institute, found that some species of grasses were successful at all altitudes, producing about 20% cover after 1 year and 50% or more after 8 years. He reported in his scientific paper in the Journal of Biogeography that common heathers regenerated quickly up to 850 metres altitude. He wrote, *"satisfactory establishment of the sown grasses at all the sites suggests that this type of restoration may be possible in other mountain restoration areas in Britain."*

Storm on the Mountain

Meanwhile, the politics in the Spey Valley rumbled on and on and one BBC TV programme tried to summarise what had been happening. Called *"Storm on the Mountain"*, it first reported that Cairngorm sold 6,500 tickets per day and had become so congested at times, as to be dangerous. Under-lining the obvious, that further development was necessary. Cairngorm was a huge success story in its time. Its problem was its own success. Adam Watson, as an advisor to the Cairngorm Board on one side, and many other bodies on the conservation side, was heavily involved in the controversy.

He took part in that programme as he did on so many similar occasions. He made the point that Cairngorm could not go on enlarging it's boundaries. To balance the story, Robert Cowan, ex Chairman of the Highlands and Islands Development Board said there was a strong case for further modest development, as into Lurcher's. And, we were reminded that the Lurcher's plan was included in the very first plans for the mountain development 30 years before. Many thought then and still think today, that using 1% of available mountain space in the Cairngorm was not unreasonable.

According to Sandy Russell, a Spey Valley councillor, again quoted in the television programme *"a lot of the conservation movement is a class movement. Some saying in effect, we want to preserve for the few and not to give it over for use by the many"*. Interesting thoughts and I seem to have heard similar voices before.

About Turn

Now, in 2011 just as I am completing the final draft for this book, comes the first indications that our climate experts are suddenly predicting that we could expect the severe cold and snowy weather we have had throughout the winters in 2010 and now into winter 2011, are expected to continue over the next decade! This was new information. Global warming has been the main topic for a decade now they talk about climate change. That has been a big turn about. Do we believe them? Can we believe them? Who do we believe?

Today we have more questions. Was the Lurcher's Gully project really a major development? The information we now have and with hind sight, it was only a minor project. A very small percentage of the entire Cairngorm region was to be involved, but it could have accommodated more skiers and relieved the congestion, the queuing times, the frustration and probably the number of skiing injuries.

Let's look at the evidence. The total area of today's Cairngorm National Park, not counting Highland Perthshire which could eventually be included, is over 3,800 square kilometres. (1,467 sq. miles)? Did I also read that the entire area utilised for downhill skiing on Cairngorm is just 2,276 acres?. Wait a moment, while I convert acres into square miles. It can't be all that large, can it? 1 square mile = 640 acres therefore, 2276 acres, etc, etc.

We should never forget or underestimate the importance of those forty Golden Years when Scotland went skiing. Tens of thousands took to the hills, most of them young people, to be challenged and to have their eyes opened to what was up there in the mountains. To feel the wind and the cold and then to welcome the sunshine and the big sky with all the elements that nature can supply. That was reality. No teacher nor any book can come close to giving that life experience. No Sunday afternoon car drive or brief trip up on the Cairngorm railway, can compensate, It is only second hand experience.

I refer to one of my own favourite books by W. H. Murray, the famous mountaineer and writer, who once wrote, *"Mountains throw into high relief a beauty that fairly takes the eye by storm … Efforts must be expended, sacrifice must be faced, without these, only imaginary mountains are climbed".*

There were more immediate problems facing those who had skis and wanted to ski in Scotland in the latter part of the twentieth century. On Cairngorm in particular, they found long queues and crowded slopes all less than appealing. The reason was, in modern jargon, under capitalisation of a dramatically growing sport and tourist industry, and the results were serious. The queue lines at chairlifts were no new phenomenon. Ski centres across the skiing world suffered from the problem from time to time. The difference between the Alpine situation and problems in Scotland lay in the overall organisation of the whole winter sports industry. In Scotland, we had a near unique situation where the majority of skiers travelled for a day or weekend of skiing. Leaving some installations to lie virtually dormant and unprofitable during the week. This was the situation at Glenshee, Glencoe and at Lecht.

Aviemore was the exception but, for some accident of history there was no direct liaison between the chairlift company and the multi million pound investments in Aviemore led by Sir Hugh Fraser in 1966. The result was the imbalance between the number of tourist beds and the uplift capacity on Cairngorm and the consequence was the growth of the lift queues. Then came the successful campaigns to stop all further skiing developments on the mountain. Then came a change in our weather patterns as snow falls became less predictable. Then there came a growing exodus to the Alps. Oh dear, Oh dear, if only… Many thousands of words, some of them highly emotional, have been written on the topic.

To help put events into perspective I should sketch out a historical timetable:

1945 Scottish National Parks Committee proposed creating national parks.

1946 Glenmore Forest Park opened to public.

1948 Glenmore Lodge opened as first mountain training centre.

1954 Cairngorms National Nature Reserve declared.

1956 Strathspey Winter Sports Development Association formed to promote skiing.

1957 Part of Cairngorm leased to the association by the Forestry Commission.

1960 Ski road built up into Coire Cas.

1961 First lifts and tows built.

1966 Aviemore Centre opened.

1967 Scottish Office published the Cairngorm Area Report outlining ski development

1968 Ptarmigan Restaurant built beside main chairlift, 400ft below summit of Cairngorm.
Ski road extended into to foot of Coire na Ciste.

1972 Forestry Commission reluctantly cede land with ski developments to HIDB.

1973 Coire na Ciste opened with car park, café and lift access to upper slopes.

1974 Countryside Commission propose special parks for Scotland. No action taken.

1976 Highland Region rejects plans that would have restricted ski development and consequently, the tourist industry.

1980 Cairngorm National Scenic Area announced.

1981 Public inquiry into proposals to extend road into Lurchers Gully and to open up the Northern Corries for skiing

The Battle of Lurchers commenced and it became ugly at times.

1990 The public inquiry and then the Scottish Office decided to oppose all attempts to extend skiing facilities.

Chapter 8

Demand for Competition

Racing Scotland

A look at the annual national ski racing calendar for 1972 demonstrates just how quickly the demand for competition had become. The Scottish Ski Club naturally was first in the field with club race events going back even before the First World War. Light hearted social events they may well have been, but the tradition was established and they are still the senior club. As the skiing movement gathered pace, competition became more and more necessary. From the mid 1960s Scottish Senior and Junior Championships sponsored by big name companies were being held on Cairngorm when the major clubs collaborated, particularly when the British Championships were held and when there was an international element. In addition to these international events there were the East, West and North Regional Senior and Junior Championships run by the Dundee, Glencoe and Aberdeen clubs. The Scottish and British Universities events were invariably held on Cairngorm and the Navy, Army and RAF held their separate annual championships. The Scottish Schools Association held individual and team championships and for

a period British Alpine Championships came on alternate years.

The Scottish Ski Club traditionally held Bairns and Junior races from early days. However, such was the demand for competition that Glencoe, Dundee and Aberdeen and Cairngorm clubs also had full race calendars and each produced British Team members who eventually gravitated into the Olympic Teams. Lothian Ski Racing Association, [LSRA] set up by volunteers initially in 1969, developed into a huge operation from 1976, using the Hillend Slope in Edinburgh. Trainees from many clubs across the central belt went through fitness and racing programmes as Hillend became the principal Scottish training hub. Han Kuwall, the Hillend Manager, took squads to his native Austria on a regular basis. He is remembered by generations of young skiers many of whom went on to the national teams.

Today, Hillend faces a difficult future as Edinburgh and Lothian Council faces financial difficulties. Nevertheless, LSRA is upbeat in campaigning to save the unique national sports facility. The 2011 update reveals that the LRSA currently has 10 trainers and 175 trainees actively involved and former LSRA trainee, Andy Noble was selected to go to the Vancouver Winter Olympics in 2010 as part of the GB team.

Schools

The early impetus for junior racing came from the great success of the Junior Alpine Test Scheme sponsored by Coca Cola. The SNSC Convenor Alick Sherriff from Perthshire reported in 1969, that there were 500 entries in the first season of operation. He praised the many schools, youth organisations and ski clubs which helped to produce that great result. The leading contributors to the scheme were Highland and Strathmore Clubs, the Scottish, Glencoe and Aberdeen clubs and the many affiliated schools including Nairn Academy, Forres Academy, Powis Secondary, Auldearn Primary, Elgin Academy, Grantown Grammer, Lossiemouth High, Perth Academy, Galashiels Academy, Gracemount Secondary and a group from the Surrey Education Authority.

Many schools within commuting distance of ski centres and plastic slopes already had skiing on their regular physical education programmes. Among the many private schools involved in the sport was Gordonstoun and just occasionally we had a glimpse of Prince Charles on Cairngorm. Alick Sherriff reckoned that there was the potential to have 8000 junior skiers in Scotland in the Test Scheme within a few years. This was just one example of how skiing gripped the nation and how it became an important "National" sport.

Throughout the 1960s, 70's and 80's when the regional race calendars were packed and entries had to be restricted, the Glencoe Club organised the West of Scotland Senior and Junior Championships. In Glenshee the Dundee Club was in charge for East of Scotland Championships, and the

Hugh Scott, a Dundee Referee

North races on Cairngorm were organised by Aberdeen.

For Scottish and British Championships and International events, all clubs pulled together with the Scottish Club playing a large part. Consequently, as a National Referee and Technical Delegate, I was drafted in to officiate at many of these events. In Glencoe I met the core members of Glencoe Ski Club and worked with them on the hill, these included Glen Perry and his son Clark who made it into the Scottish and British Teams. Laurie Robertson and I worked together on SNSC committees, and I knew Chris Lyon and other original Glencoe Ski Club worthies. Of course, I also met my counterparts from the other clubs on many occasions.

Over many years the average ski season could last for four months and accordingly, race meetings were scheduled for every weekend. There were some weather cancellations of course but remarkably, most events did go ahead or were re-scheduled. This calendar illustrates how packed the calendar was, in just six years after the Ski Council was up and running and racing had become formalised.

Scottish Race Calendar 1971

January

8/9	Hillender EC	Hillend
15	Snowmaster Bearsden S.C.	Cairngorm
16	Giant Slalom Scottish S.C.	Glenshee
16	Gulabin GS Dundee G.S.	Glenshee
23	Dundee/ Aberdeen GS	Glenshee
30	Scottish Universities	Glenshee
30	Glencoe GS	Glencoe
30	Swallow Slalom Aberdeen	Glenshee

February

5/6	East of Scot. Seniors Dundee SC	Glenshee
5/6	North of Scot. Juniors	Cairngorm
12/13	Spittal Quaich Dundee SC	Glenshee

20	MackayAberdeen SC	Glenshee
19/20	Scot Univ. SUSC	Cairngorm
26	Schools Challenge	Glenshee
26/27	North of Scot Seniors Aberdeen SC	Cairngorm
26/27	West of Scot Juniors Glencoe SC	Glencoe

March

5	Tennant Trophy Scottish SC	Glenshee
12	National Schools Races	Glenshee
16/18	Army Ski Assoc. Championships	Cairngorm
26	Hird Trophy Scottish SC	Cairngorm

April

6/9	Scottish Junior Champs	Cairngorm
10/13	British Universities Champs	Cairngorm
11	Scottish Ladies Champs.	Cairngorm
14/20	British Alpine and Scottish Championships SNSC	
		Cairngorm
23	Coronation Cup Scottish SC	Cairngorm
29	Highland Pentathlon	Aviemore

These races, in many instances, were oversubscribed and start lists had to be limited. In 1972 the British Alpine Championship came to Scotland for only the second time, the first being in 1967 when foreign currency restrictions were severe and inhibited foreign travel. The '72 British six day event on Cairngorm was sponsored by Inghams Travel and subsidised by the Scottish Tourist Office It was the first time that the event had been listed on the FIS Calendar, consequently, several world class names appeared on the start lists from Austria, France, Switzerland and Norway. Among the men were Alain Benz [Fra] B. Charvin [Fra] J. Odermatt [Swit] and the women, Odile Chalvin [Fra] Florence Steurer [Fra] Ellen Vangen [Nor]. The British events were held in April when all international races in the Alps had finished and it was always possible for the international skiers to improve their seed points in Scotland.

Blood on the Snow

The Chief of Course at one British Championship event was from the Aberdeen Club and he and his team were under pressure to build double race courses for the Slalom, so that there would be no delay between the end of the first run and the start of the second.

That day, the second run started promptly with no delays. The first time it had happened at any major championship! Bonus points for the Aberdeen Club! Up to 90 seeded racers could be involved in these races and start officials and referees were under pressure to speed up the action. Even with one minute start intervals, it only took a couple of racers to "wipe out" and demolish a section of the course, to cause lengthy delays.

The passage of many skis inevitably cut up the surface of the course which needed frequent repair by officials side-slipping down the affected sections to smooth out the ruts. At times, when snow cover was thin, extra snow would be shovelled into place to fill bare patches or to cover exposed rocks. Races had to be halted briefly to allow these repairs to be carried out.

Normally, at such big race meetings, it was a race against time to groom and set the second course. The first race course could be prepared, racing poles dispersed down the course the evening before, ready for an early start by the course setter. To build a second course after the first leg was a race against the clock. It required a squad of skiers who were not involved in running the first leg race and had the ability to carry large bundles of seven foot ash poles and flags, up and down a hill, on skis ready for a new course setter to construct his course. When that was done, a Technical Delegate, a foreign official when there was an international element to the event, had to inspect the course to approve its suitability.

National pride was always at stake for these were big international events, supported by major sponsors and covered by the national press. Club pride was also an issue because there was always a certain amount of "wha's best, east or west". Frith Finlayson, a professional instructor on this occasion was not involved in the organisation but had been a Chief of Course at a past event. He was working on the hill with his instructors and a disagreement

broke out and "words" were exchanged with the Course Chief of the day, over the disputed ownership of a batch of race poles.

Frith reacted, as I say, for he could be fiery, and the duty "Chief" over reacted and the two came very close to fisticuffs. Both had kicked off their skis and were set to have a punch up in the middle of the White Lady ski slope. A neutral figure, I think a past President of the Scottish Ski Club, happened on the scene and stood between the protagonists and defused the situation. As I say, the stakes were high and the pressure was on for everyone. I personally was very glad that neutral person came to calm down the situation, because, it could have been my blood on the snow that day.

Tale of the Frozen Gatekeeper

Thought also had to be given to the gatekeepers, the long suffering officials who have to stick to their posts whatever the delays and whatever the weather conditions. For Giant Slalom, perhaps 15 volunteers would be spaced over the long course, pencil and pads at the ready, to note any infringements at their appointed gates. A thankless task, lightened perhaps by the appointed Chief Gatekeeper who was required to feed and water them at intervals and, in extreme weather conditions, to check that they were still at their posts or even still alive.

Being a gatekeeper on a Scottish mountain was not always a pleasant job and officials had to resort to blackmail or coercion at times. If the wind was biting and the temperature low, some experienced keepers would dig out a hollow and build a snow wall to give some shelter. Others preferred to keep moving and the real old hands would take the precautions of wearing long johns and several layers of clothing. A hardy breed indeed! With a wry smile, I turn to a piece from one ski club magazine in 1963.

Definition of Exposure

This is not a strict medical term but in general it describes the serious effects from exposure to climatic hazards. It is in general limited to the effects of cold environments. Phrases frequently include "risk of exposure" and " death by exposure". In other words, a reduction in the heat content of the body. So, a definition of exposure is severe chilling of the body surface, leading to a progressive fall in body temperature with the risk of death from hypothermia.

We Chief Gatekeepers of course, never relayed this definition of "exposure" to those we bullied into standing on a mountain in Scotland for several hours at a time. To my knowledge no one died from hypothermia whilst gate keeping —— at least, not on my watch! At large junior events, keepers were easier to find, for parents often volunteered for duty particularly on good days. At senior races it became necessary on occasion to require competitors to supply a gatekeeper, either a family member or friend. At international races at world level when top skiers are in fact professional, gatekeepers are paid. We never quite reached that level of sophistication in Scotland.

At one British International Championships held on Cairngorm it was decided to enlist the help of the Royal Marine 45 Commando based in Arbroath. The particular unit detailed off to assist in the championships had just returned from arctic training in Norway and a five day deployment on Cairngorm was no hardship. While they were trained to ski, they had no experience of downhill racing and it's organisation. My job included spending an evening with the detachment at their Kingussie winter depot, the week before the races. With demonstration boards and slides, I passed on the basics of gate-keeping. During the five day race meeting, the lads also assisted in course preparation and they all did a good job, contributing greatly to the overall success of the championships.

Homologation

New race courses were created by the Cairngorm Company and homologated by the ruling body, the Federation International d'Ski, who sent Roland Rudin from Grindelwald in Switzerland. When it became news that Cairngorm was to be "Homologated" there was some consternation among Scottish skiers. It was a new term and we didn't quite know what to expect. Was it bad news? Was it against the law? Was it a notice to quit? It turned out to be good news, for it was the first in Scotland at that time, to be registered. Glenshee was next when the Cairnwell with its Tiger Piste was also to be ratified. Actually, it only meant that any new race course was confirmed as being of the correct length, the appropriate steepness and etc., for international seed points to be awarded by the FIS.

Technology

In the early days, communications between the start position and the finish gate was by landline and, if the cable was cut by clumsy skiers, long delays occurred. Gradually the technology improved, communications were radio controlled, finish gates operated by electronic beams and times, to 100th of a second, were recorded automatically in a timing hut where the boffins worked. Long gone were the days of the hand-held stop watches.

In spring conditions, granular snow was easily swept aside by the racing skiers and when necessary, hydroscopic agricultural salt was used to stabilise it. This entailed course workers skiing downhill with sacks of salt to sprinkle at vulnerable points on the course. Then the salt was raked into the snow. It was messy work and ruinous to leather gloves but, it did work and gave racers a firmer and more consistent racing surface.

The British Championships in 1972 was a huge event supported by the whole Spey Valley with added sponsorship by Highlands & Islands Development Board. In the FIS report after the event, much was said about the efficiency of the Scottish organisation especially in the face of "challenging" conditions. We "workers on the hill" knew all about that! In the following year the British Championships went to France and significantly, the appointed Chief of the Championships was Jim Gellatly, the Dundee Club Race Convenor. The report also said that there was every likelihood that Scotland would be asked to stage a European Cup event in the not too distant future.

But I'm the referee!

Chapter 9

Racing People

Hot Competition

As commercial sponsorship began to kick in, 1966 was a pivotal year when the first of the "local loons" in the Spey Valley gained meaningful sponsorship. Tomatin Distillers were the first to present the Scottish National Ski Council with a ski scholarship of £600 which was awarded to Rory Macleod of Rothiemurcus in Invernesshire. He had been equal first with Luke O'Reilly at the British Junior Championships held in Andermatt that year, and was the first Scot to achieve that ranking.

Richard Callingham, Tomatin Distillers chairman gave the news at the company's annual general meeting in London and he underlined that the scholarship was intended to assist the training at home and abroad, of a Scottish skier who would be available for training up to British national team standard. Rory lived at that time by the road up to Cairngorm and he was one of the Red Devils of the Spey Valley who spent much of their time when out of school, on the mountain, while some of them went on to become ski instructors.

Young Peter Fuchs, son of Karl the ski teacher, had a low profile in his early years, but, in 1968 at one Scottish Junior Championships the name P. Fuchs appeared on the start lists. The race organising fraternity knew Karl had family but we had not seen the boy because he had not come up through the Bairn's and Junior ranks and we had no idea of his standard. The seeding system was still in its infancy and in that event he came from the back of the field to finish in the first group. The crafty Karl Fuchs had groomed his only son before launching him into the race circuit where he made an immediate impact.

A very young Konrad Bartelski racing on Cairngorm

Ce n'est pas possible ... c'est un Anglais

Peter Fuchs met Konrad Bartelski at a subsequent junior race meeting in Scotland and the two became close friends who were to dominate in British Teams, for some years. Konrad was schooled for a while in Scotland and raced frequently on the junior circuits. I was referee at a number of these junior events when both boys raced and it was a joy to follow their progress up into the senior ranks, the British Team and onto the world stage.

Konrad had several top ten results but his most outstanding result was in World Cup Downhill at Val Gardena in the Italian Dolomites. It was on 11th. December 1981 when he was just 11 hundredths of a second behind the winner. Viewers of Ski Sunday that day saw his magnificent run on one of the toughest downhill courses on the World circuit. The French commentator exploded in amazement and shouted, *"Ce n'est pas possible ... c'est un Anglais"* ... It can't be ... it's an Englishman.

Well actually, we claimed Konrad for Scotland, because many of the earliest influences in his young skiing career, took place on Scottish snow. Konrad retired in 1983 after three Olympic Winter Games and went on to carve out new careers, firstly commentating for Ski Sunday and various sports programmes before becoming a director of a major sports equipment company.

Later he became Chairman of the British Ski and Snowboard Federation, the very organisation which sacked or de-listed him from the British Team for being incompatible with team policy toward the end of his racing career. Having dual nationality, Konrad joined the Dutch Team for a season as if to cock a snoop at the British establishment. In 2010 he again had issues with the Federation which by this time he actually chaired. To his astonishment and to the nation as a whole, Snowsport GB ran out of money and pulled the plug on all funding for the Winter Olympic Teams preparing to compete in Vancouver in February 2010, and went into administration.

Konrad's comments at that time suggested that it was the best thing that could happen to British Skisport and that there was no doubt in his mind who was to blame for the current crisis. *"It was time to start afresh"* he said. It seems that in this new century there could still be too many cooks running British skiing. Back in time, in 1977, the same problem had occurred in London and simmered on for ages. Out of the blue, the news came that the British Ski Teams were to be called home prematurely from the World Cup and European circuits in January that year.

The news came from General Ian Graeme, the Alpine Controller and Secretary of the National Ski Federation of Great Britain. The sudden recall of the British Team as the season had hardly begun and the alarming financial deficit, caused more than a little surprise in Scotland. More so because our officials had not been consulted nor had been party to the decision to recall the national racers. The Scots had from the beginning, been critical of organisation and budgeting in London. The SNSC claimed that the teams had been sent to the Alps without adequate management and on shoestring budgets, with constant calls for extra support from the parents and clubs of team members.

Konrad & Peter

The Scottish racing clubs were also aware that they had contributed 50% or more, towards the British Olympic Appeal Funds in 1976, which, on a population per capita basis, reflected very, very badly on their English counterparts. When contacted, Lewis Grant of Grantown on Spey, the Scottish race convenor and also a member of the British Alpine Committee based in London, knew nothing of the proposed withdrawal of the national squad and less of the financial mess. Less diplomatic Scottish officials were more scathing and talked of, *"yet another breakdown in communications between London and Scotland. Despite repeated calls from the SNSC and from parents of Team members, the National Ski Federation of GB, had failed to complete the accounts for the season 1976 and for the Olympic Games held in Innsbruck".*

Plunging Pound

That summer the Minister for Sport, Dennis Howell, called for post-Olympic talks with all the amateur sports bodies in Britain. When skiing interests were called to discuss matters with the Sports Minister, no Scottish officials were present. The result was predictable comments north of the border. There was anger and calls for more autonomy for the sport in Scotland. Admittedly, there were other reasons the British teams had financial problems. Inflation was one cause because the pound was worth 42 Austrian Schillings in 1976 and in 1977 the rate had plunged to 28 Schillings.

The British Federation had an annual grant of £25,000 from the Sports Council, in addition, two major sponsors donated £2,500 each and gave the Team the use of four estate cars for the entire season. A further £30,000 in ski equipment was gifted by a pool of manufacturers. Perhaps a little belt tightening by those in charge would have allowed the teams to have more time on Alpine snow that winter.

The Scottish National Ski Council had been formed to avoid any interference from London and was largely able to do so. The very existence of the SNSC was a thorn in the flesh of the London based traditionalists but the Scottish clubs were too busy helping to nurture the skiing revolution in Scotland

Ian Cairns president of the Scottish Ski Club and his daughter Kirstin. British Team member and Olympian.

to get involved in London politics. In the space of five years our own Ski Council set up in 1963, represented 60 ski clubs with 10,000 active skiers, soon to grow to 14.000. In addition we had created a racing circuit of regional and national, senior and junior championship events and gathered an impressive number of major companies to sponsor race events and to contribute in a major way towards a junior training programme. We were also better at budgeting.

Hamish Liddell of Pitlochry who was Chairman and President of SNSC, insisted that our sponsors put 50% of their sponsorships funding into our junior training schemes. There was some resistance because sponsors who are seldom philanthropists, preferred to wine and dine dignitaries, officials and the press. But the SNSC stuck to its principles which were that funding for the next generation was the way forward for Scottish Skiing. This system worked quite dramatically as witness the success of Scots at regional and British events. From the late 1960s Scots skiers began to dominate in British ski sport. Slowly but surely, Scots names came to the fore and this was simply because of forward planning, good accounting and, the backing of many important sponsors.

The Bell Boys

Martin Bell from Ediburgh was academically very clever and completed his formal education in a Swiss sports academy. In his second year there, he fell and had a serious knee injury, not skiing related, which needed ligament surgery carried out by a famous ski injury specialist based in Innsbruck.

That was Martin out for the 1981-82 season. His first World Cup downhill saw him finish in 45th place but over two more seasons he crept up the charts. By 1986 with British team reorganisation and training and contact with the N. American teams which included the two Canadian Crazy Cannucks, Ken Read and Todd Brooker, Martin made his first breakthrough with his 10th place at Val Gardena in the Dolomites. That earned him his first World Cup points, 6 precious points and a place in the top ten. From the first group in any race it was always possible to ski into the top three and that could mean in medal terms, Bronze, Silver or Gold.

Martin Bell, the British No.1

Graham Bell

There was more good news, this time about Lesley Beck from Dumbarton who came second in the Noram Slalom Championships in Vermont USA. Like Martin Bell she was heading for the coveted points in World Cup. Her nick name? "Scotland's Mighty Mouse". Graham Bell and Ron Duncan from Edinburgh were both in the British Team at this time and despite injuries both had tantalising glimpses of great success, racing in World Cup. Since retiring in 1998 Graham went on to make a name in television as a presenter on Ski Sunday and to present the 2010 Winter Olympics for BBC.

Golden Coffee Beans

World Cup Alpine Racing was serious stuff and sponsors almost fought amongst themselves to have their brand name at the top of the list. The new World Cup sponsor in 1987 was Lavazza Coffee and the new currency in ski sport became the gold plated coffee bean where those racers placed in the first 15 in world ranking got these gold plated beans in number equal to the points they won: One for fifteenth place, 25 beans for first place. Italy's Albert Tomba had a big, big bag of beans to jingle, while Scotland's first lady, Lesley Beck had but three ... at that time. She had worked hard for them on the world stage.

There were six Scots in the British Squad in 1976 under the direction of Dieter Bartsch an Austrian coach. It was significant also that both British Alpine titles were held by Scots. Peter Fuchs of Carrbridge was Men's Champion and the Women's title was held by Hazel Hutcheon of Dundee. Anne Robb of Aberdeen Ski Club held the British Slalom title and was runner up to Hazel in the combined championships. Anne was selected for the UK Olympic Team to Innsbruck in 1976 when just sixteen and again to Lake Placid in 1980. It was always my pleasure to recall these young Scottish skiers, for my generation saw them all coming up through the ranks. Anne's school put pressure on her to play Saturday school hockey instead of skiing and I was asked to write to the Head Mistress to make her aware of Anne's potential. That potential was a place in the Winter Olympics.

British Women's Ski Team, 1976, which includes Hazel Hutcheon of Dundee 2nd left, Catherine Leggat of Edinburgh 4th left and Anne Robb of Aberdeen 5th left. Team captain Valentina Cliffe is far right.

Princess Micheal of Kent, Lesley Beck and John Ritblat at the British Alpine Championships in Sils, Switzerland.

Anne Robb, Aberdeen Olympic skier

Crazy Canucks

At the other end of the spectrum, I was reporting results of an international event on Cairngorm featuring a downhiller called Ken Read, a Canadian skier who was a star in World Cup and a Olympic medallist. He had come to Scotland at the end of his international season, on a promotional visit and to race for the first time on Scottish snow. On this big occasion I had the chance to report events to a number of papers including the Guardian and I got my fingers burnt, simply by spelling the winner's name incorrectly!

The name was Read, not Reid. The duty sports editor rang me to point out my error and I had to grovel and promise to be more careful in future. Ironically, the Guardian Newspaper at that time was going through a period when spelling mistakes on every page were frequent, and commented about in the industry. Read was one of the "Crazy Canucks", a winning squad of Canadian Team skiers and he won two Olympic medals in his illustrious career then went on to sit on F.I.S. committees before being made a member of the Order of Canada. The last I heard, he was co-owner of a major Canadian ski resort. Success breeds success.

In those days, news reports were telephoned in by the reporter on the spot and taken down by a copy typist so, there was always a chance of a spelling mistake. Today, all journalists type up their own copy and send it electronically to the editorial desk, with less likelihood of error. I was in the pre-electronic age and today I still struggle to understand what my "mouse" is doing. I did not have too many opportunities to report for the Guardian newspaper because the Sports Editor was John Samuel, a giant in the newspaper industry who had a particular interest in ski sport. I also rubbed shoulders with John Hennessey who had been sports editor at the Times for 25 years before semi-retiring and covering ice skating and skiing. He subsequently wrote a successful book about Jayne Torvill and Christopher Dean after their "Bolero" Olympic success.

Lesley Beck, the Dumbarton Mighty Mouse

Ron Duncan, British Downhiller, Edinburgh

Scottish Senior Alpine Championships of Cairngorm April 1976
Left to Right: Peter Fuchs, Carrbridge; Andrew Begg, Eligin; Clarke Perry, East Kilbride;
Sponsor; Jim Currie, Chairman, Scottish National Ski Council; Sponsor; Jane Allison,
Edinburgh; Hazel Hutcheon, Dundee.
Kneeling in Front: Scottish Champions. Alan Stewart, North Queensferry; and Anne
Robb, Aberdeen.

Not Just Downhill

By the early1970s Freestyle skiing had become a new kid on the block with the
early emphasis moving towards mogul runs and parallel slalom. These two
particular events were closer to traditional competition. Freestyle on the other
hand was more informal as the individualists carried out the most astonishing
aerial acrobatics. The SNSC set up freestyle camps for both amateurs and
professionals as it was important that expert and safe advice guided budding
athletes. The Scottish Amateur Freestyle Championships were set up by the

SNSC with help from the Scottish Club and sponsorship from Famous Grouse. A dual slalom circuit was included by popular demand with races at Cairngorm and Glenshee for it was always a great spectacle to watch.

Dual and even Triple slalom events were already being held across the country on snow and on plastic dry ski slopes. Freestyle first became an Olympic Sport in 1992 in Albertville when mogul skiing was adopted. Aerials followed in Lilliehammer in Norway, which was held just two years after the 1992 Games, as decreed by the IOC to avoid the Summer and Winter Games falling in the same years.

Viewing the Vancouver Games in 2010, I was captivated by the new types of skiing being introduced for the first time. Ski Cross is the event where the competitors fling themselves off the starting platform and pile downhill, four abreast. The battle is to get on the inside line for the first corner and to cope with massive jumps at the same time. Alpine Downhill speed is insane but Ski Cross is even more exciting and certainly gets the spectator's blood going. There is no timing; it is first past the post with the first two in each round going forward to quarter, semi and final rounds. Downhill is still the tough race in Alpine events but could we see the likes of Ski Cross with its head to head racing, becoming the next top event?

Rebuke

Being just an old, old-fashioned skier I got my fingers rapped when I attempted to describe the new freestyle developments. In a Scotsman article some 25 years ago entitled "Proper Sport or Spectacle", I questioned whether freestyle was a competitive sport in the accepted sense, or an acrobatic spectacle packaged to attract media exposure. I was sharply rebuked by Sara Ferguson, then Chairperson of the British Ski Federation Freestyle Committee. She wrote a stiff letter in the letters to the Editor. saying, *"This may not be clear to him, (that's me) but it is to the International Ski Federation {FIS} who recognised freestyle in 1980 as an amateur sport ... For the past four years the British championships have been held in Scotland ... and the sport is on the short list to be accepted at the 1988 Winter Games. With 17 nations competing in the FIS World Cup, Britain is among the leaders with European champion Mike Nemesvary from Paisley, ranked fourth in the combined. Robin Wallace second at ballet in international youth level, is one of our Gold Medal hopes for the first freestyle world championships."*

Mike Nemesvary never competed in the World Championships for he suffered a horrendous accident in 1985. Practising on a trampoline in his own back garden, he fell and broke his neck and severed his spine. The 24 year old was wheel chair bound but such was his resolution to get on with his life, within eight months of injury he headed for Tignes in France with a specially designed toboggan, to be filmed by a Channel 4 film crew who recorded his months since the accident. In his days as the master of freestyle skiing he appeared in the Bond film, "A View to a Kill" when he carried out a spectacular stunt in the opening sequences. Following his accident he launched a new charity called "Back Up" with Barbara Broccoli the 25 year old daughter of the film producer Cubby Broccoli, to help spinal injury victims.

British International Freestyle Team 1988

Dressed for Speed

Speed Skiing ... In Scotland?

Everyone loves a little speed in their lives. It gives us a kick, an adrenalin buzz but big time speed skiing is something else. I mean, can we even begin to imagine what it would feel like to achieve 200kph ... on skis? Even more astonishing was the fact that one leg of the World Speed Championships sponsored by Smirnoff was held in Glenshee in 1985. No notable speeds were recorded simply because, predictably, the weather with high winds ruined the day. Franz Weber of Austria with his 208.92kph.world record was there with two Scots members of his team, Alan "Midge" White from Edinburgh and John Clark from Aviemore, both had notable times in a notoriously dangerous sport with ultimate challenge.

The speed seeker squads then moved to Les Arc in France which is reputed to have the world's fastest track. The proponents wore skin tight, low friction catsuits with aerodynamic helmets based on those worn by the TV Dhark Vader character. The two Scots had first made their marks in Scottish Alpine race events and later moved on to the British teams, both racing and in coaching. In 1987 the speed record was broken again this time by Frenchman Michel Prufer, in Chile with 217 kph. He had earlier snatched the world record from Graham Wilkie of Guildford. John Clark had earlier moved up to 193kph, then to 200kph and then in South America he topped 205kph, his personal best. He had been hotly tipped on that occasion but a dramatic mistake in his final run knocked him out of contention.

Describing the action John, then aged 26 and a director of the Lecht Ski

Graham Wilkie of Guildford

School, said, *"On the critical run I chose a different line over new snow. At about 200kph my skis started to float and I drifted across old tracks, hit a bump and my skis popped apart just as I hit the 100metre speed trap. Otherwise I could have been in the top three".* Doing the splits when skiing can be, to say the least, painful. But, at 200kph. Wow. There were competing sponsored teams all attempting to break the records and the International Ski Federation had refused to ratify the speed records preferring to leave the rival camps dominated by commercial interests to make claim and counter-claim. Only Japan, Austria, the USA,. Italy, France and Britain at that time had produced record holders in the previous 50 years.

Speed skiing in Scotland did not finish there. Kerr Blyth of Edinburgh became the new holder of the Scottish Speed Skiing record in 1991. The student better known as a top seed in slalom, pushed the record up to 154.74 kph on the new course on Aonach Mor by Fort William. He led the joint Glasgow/Strathclyde University to the team title with Heriot Watt University second and Aberdeen University third. He broke the Scottish record set three years before in Glenshee. The optimistic organiser, John Wilson, said the Nevis Range track could produce speeds of over 200kph and an international FIS race later that year could see the break through. It did not happen, the reason? The weather!

Cross Country

The Pentlands and the Ochill hills attracted many early skiers back in the 1950s because they were within a tram/bus ride of the cities. At the height of the "Glory Days" in the 1960s and 70's, there was also a rapid increase in those who preferred the hills rather than the increasingly crowded ski centres. Sales of cross country skis and boots rocketed as more and more headed out to the vast arctic plateau lying between Cairngorm and Ben Macdhui and so many other lonely mountains. Later, on lower hills, cross country trails were opened up by the Forestry Commission in the Clashindarroch Forest by Huntly, in the Angus Glens and near Tomintoul. Today, some official biking trails are kept open for skiers when snow covered.

The beauty of the nearby at Tyrebagger Hill six miles from Aberdeen.

Alternative Sports

The first attempts to use skis in the mountains by my generation, were purely utilitarian and only to allow us to get from mountain to mountain. There was no specialist equipment, no finesse, nothing which could be classified as Langlauf , Cross Country or Ski Mountaineering style. Things have moved on as equipment developed and today in rural Aberdeenshire there is a very large forestry area dedicated to Nordic Ski Sports on snow tracks maintained by trail cutters. There is more than 14 kilometres of forest tracks maintained for skiers and in recent years there has been an average of 45 snow skiing days available. While in 2010 they had 106 days open to the public. The snow gone, the tracks are then open to mountain bikers and runners.

The adjoining Huntly Nordic and Outdoor Centre has a 800 metre tarmac roller ski track, a 400 metre classic dry XC track, a tubing downhill mat, all purpose built, all-weather facilities. The Centre is operated by Grampian Region and in 2004 a Lottery grant allowed major up-grading. The Huntly Nordic Club were already producing athletes who compete at national and international level. With no snow, roller skiing really is the next best thing and a major training facility for X-C fanatics. By the 1980s the Association of Nordic Ski Instructors had amalgamated with the British Association of Ski Instructors and this entirely logical move brought Britain into line with other skiing nations, whereby one umbrella organisation was responsible for the training and grading of instructors in both Alpine and Nordic disciplines.

By 1985 there were active groups in some of the most unusual areas of the UK as this list of member clubs indicates: Manchester X-C Ski Club, Hexham X-C Ski Club, Lakeland X-C Ski Club, London Region X-C Ski Clu,. Newcastle University X-C Club, Sheffield X-C Club, Susnord X-C Clu,. Tyneside Loipers and Yorkshire Dales X-C Club. In Scotland active clubs operated in Edinburgh, Aberdeen, Glasgow, Ross-shire, Strathspey and Tayside. If you are a hill person you will have admired the work of Cameron McNeish, that prolific writer of mountain books and the television presenter who has introduced countless folk to the mountains. In 1984 a younger Cameron contributed to the Nordic Ski Yearbook with some essential information about the gear needed for that branch of snowsport.

Prehistoric bindings circa 1952

Basic XC

Profile

Any Spey Valley edition of "Who's Who," would describe this subject as: *Born Edinburgh 1942: ex-British team skier; prominent ski instructor: BASI coach and examiner; Ex-British Freestyle Champion; Other interests, Knitting.* In order to clear up that last point, I should tell the tale of the woollen hat Kenny Dickson bought in Wengen in 1970 where he was instructing. It was much admired when he went back home and he had a few replicas knitted up by a friend. These sold well and a professional machine was used to start a business selling the hats to friends, ski schools, sponsors, and the public.

Like topsy that small business expanded to complement his ski instructing career. Tentative selling expeditions brought more orders and when he first designed his Union Jack hat it sold like hot cakes. A visit to Japan to the World Interski Conference in 1977 saw Kenny as a member of the highly acclaimed British Association of Ski Instructors demonstration team. He took time out to establish sales outlets for his growing range of products. A number of British climbing expeditions were kitted out with the red, white and blue hats including the fateful Chris Bonington Everest Expedition where photographer Mike Burke was lost on the summit ridge ... wearing the hat.

It was his local Scout Group in Edinburgh which first introduced Kenny to skiing at Glenshee in 1959. By 1963 he was racing in the embryo Scottish circuit and then with a £200 grant award he headed to the Alps and the British Championships in Davos. By one more year he moved to a caravan in Aviemore to train as an instructor and worked for two years at the Frith Finlayson Ski School d'Ecosse. Passing the BASI grade 1 exams he headed to Wengen and the headquarters of the Downhill Only Ski Club where he taught the distinctive Dickson style. Then came partnership with Hans Kuwall and Tony Wimmer in the highly successful Cairngorm Ski Racing

School. The school trained many of the emerging stars of Scottish skiing who went on the become members of the British Teams.

By the mid 1970s after ten or more years instructing, his knitting business was beginning to offer some security for the future, but he was aware that some of the kick was going out his skiing. That was when Freestyle hit Scotland. It put life back into the sport for many and Kenny found the discipline and the keen competitive edge just what he needed. He lifted the British Freestyle title in 1975 and again, in the big year 1977, when Colgate splashed a lot of money into sponsorship. Kenny took most of the prize money and his 2nd British title. He told me once that he didn't know anything about knitting … he only really knew about skiing. Did I tell you how I had watched him skiing down the White Lady on a quiet day, to the music of the Samba? Poetry in motion!

Kenny Dickson, the Hat Man

Another Record

The entire British landscape was turned into a winter playground in 1982 … but few skiers were able to ski simply because they got stuck on motorways and in snow drifts just trying to reach chairlift country. Only a few, the cross country skiers, were able to take full advantage. One group of super men did just that, to make the first continuous ski traverse of Scotland. Admittedly, it was across the shortest point from west to east but they did it in just 14 hours and, it was a record. Tim Walker, Keith Geddes, Blyth Wright and Sam Crymble set off from Loch Duich at 7am on January 13th and arrived at Beauly at midnight the same day. The group were all instructors at Glenmore Lodge and at one point they skied right down the middle of frozen Loch Affric. Keith Geddes, who was a Scottish Junior Team Trainer, said at the end of the trek, "Probably the most difficult part of the whole journey was trying to get out of the pub at Cannich where we stopped for a break"

The Scottish Haute Route

Harold Raeburn in the 1905 Scottish Mountaineering Club Journal wrote of his love of winter climbing but he dismissed out of hand the possibility of finding skis of much use in Scottish conditions.

"I consider skis will but seldom be used in Scotland with advantage and enjoyment. The condition and amount of snow even on our hills is not often likely to be suitable. On the low ground at any rate in the neighbourhood of Edinburgh and Glasgow, we have many winters with practically no snow. On the hills it is usually, if not soft and sticky, hard and icy. Seldom do we find the dry white powder characteristics of Norwegian winter snow. In exceptional frosts and exceptional seasons, such as at intervals of ten years or so, we may have opportunities to safe practice, but to become adept, and to enjoy this most interesting and fascinating sport to perfection we must visit countries less under the influence of Atlantic mildness and moisture than is our native land."

Despite what that famous early Scottish climber had to say over a hundred years ago, ski mountaineering did become possible and popular. As modern equipment became available the options opened up for everyone and today, many have dreams of tackling the big winter mountain journeys. The Classic Haute Route from Chamonix to Zermatt is indeed a classic and has been done many times. But the challenges here in Scotland can be just as rigorous as described in the article in the Scottish Mountaineering Club Journal by David Grieve in 1978.

His companions were Sandy Cousins, Derek Pyper and Mike Taylor, the latter I had first met at the World Scout Jamboree in France in 1947. David Grieve I knew through the Aberdeen Club when he won an early cross country race and served for a time on committee. Together with these three companions, he decided to tackle a northern route which took in the more challenging terrain thought to be truly deserving of the title of the Scottish Haute Route. They planned for a six day trip but it turned out to be seven days when they staggered into the Glen Nevis youth hostel in Fort William. Starting in Glen Gairn near Ballater, they depended on mountain bothies but were equipped to bivouac in an emergency, consequently they carried heavier loads than is necessary in the Alps where well equipped mountain refuges are common place. In comparison with the classic Haute Route from Chamonix to Zermatt the distances were greater in the Scottish Route but the heights climbed were broadly comparable.

Chapter 10

The Spey Valley

The Aviemore Centre

Shortly after the Cairngorm Chairlift Company, began operations in 1961, government encouraged a consortium of businessmen to help stem the drift of population from the Highlands. Lord Fraser of Allander, founder of the drapery empire, House of Fraser and, Sir William McEwan Younger were members of the original consortium which conceived the Centre. Sir William went on to become chairman of the Highland Tourist Board.

Until the Centre became established, Aviemore had a population of 580. In ten years this had grown to 1,500 and was still growing. New shops, business premises, craft and light industries, a school, police and fire stations all appeared. Local authorities and private builders built over 300 houses and local hotels and guest houses were upgraded to cope with the all-year-round trade. Aviemore became popular as a major conference centre hosting everyone from the World Forum of the Aberdeen Angus Cattle Society, to the Medical Profession of the United States with 900 delegates.

1976 saw the first international charter flights from Scandanavia to Inverness, linking to Aviemore and the reputation of the Spey Valley grew rapidly. The international sized ice rink hosted major curling tournaments and even ice hockey teams sprang up, while the swimming pool was always hugely popular. A second ice rink was built by the Coylumbridge Hotel with 500 beds and all these facilities meant that whatever the weather on Cairngorm, there was always lots to do.

Kangaroo Valley

With the Centre and other hotels over a wide area, recording great business, more staff were required and this was when Spey Valley was renamed Kangaroo Valley, because young Antipodeans were flocking to find seasonal work. Australians in particular were and still are, great travellers and a newspaper report in 1974 confirmed that there were 160 employed in hotels, pubs and shops in the Spey Valley, 70 of them at the Aviemore Centre alone. Australians and New Zealanders after the war began to get the wanderlust to visit their early family homelands. They first headed for Earls Court and Kensington districts in London which became known as London's Kangaroo Valley but soon the majority were bypassing the big city to travel directly to Spey Valley where there was always a great deal of work available and, it had good skiing, while the Aviemore Centre had first class recreational facilities including swimming and skating. Mr. Sandy Caird, owner of the largest and first established sports shop in the Centre, with branches around Scotland said at the time, "Aviemore could not operate without the Aussies … they are a great bunch".

Phoenix Rises

It was a boom time for some 20 years but slowly and surely the clock ticked on. More skiers chose to fly abroad to ski and weather patterns changed. The numbers coming to the Spey Valley diminished, jobs were lost, and generally, business declined. The Aviemore Centre was unable to move with the times and lacked capital investment. First the swimming pool closed then the curling rink, shops closed and hotels struggled as the boom times ended. Skiing had been the original catalyst, the essential component which allowed Aviemore to flourish and grow into an all-season resort. Gradually as snowfalls became more erratic and failed at times, the foundations crumbled.

Today it is all change. Gone is the doom and gloom as the Phoenix rises and the new Aviemore is adapting to the changing times. New facilities are coming onstream, the old are being refurbished and re-invented. While the numbers skiing in Scotland has been in slow decline, water and other sports have increased in the Spey Valley and one development in particular has caught the imagination of many. Clive Freshwater had been an instructor at Glenmore Lodge but he had a dream to start his own business in the Spey Valley. To achieve that he had to fight a major legal battle with local vested interests, government agencies and bloody mindedness. But more of that later.

The Highland Pentathlon

One spin off from the skiing movement and developments on Cairngorm was the John Player Highland Pentathlon held in Aviemore at the end of each ski season. It was the brain child of Capt. Wells, the Managing Director of the original centre, just a year after it opened in 1966. It brought together, what became the most diverse assembly of sports enthusiasts and teams, gathered anywhere in the United Kingdom. The original Greek Olympic Pentathlon, comprised running, jumping, wrestling, discus and javelin throwing and it was their expression of what the complete athlete in that age should be. The translation of the Modern Pentathlon events into Highland terms was a happy inspiration. Two events, swimming and running were common to both, and the balance between skill and stamina was maintained in the skiing, curling and shooting competitions. The Highland Pentathlon inevitably attracted teams from the many ski clubs across Britain and it tended to be ski clubs which carried off the trophies.

The event proved to be for a special kind of person, the all-rounders who could make a good account of him/her self in several fields although they may not be outstanding in any one. Covering three days, the competitors were housed in the chalet village of the Centre. Teams booked in on Friday evenings when the team briefings took place. Competition began at 8.30 am on Saturday with the swimming, followed by the giant slalom on Cairngorm and in the evening, target curling at the

Aviemore International Curling Rink. Sunday morning saw the 25 metre small bore shooting followed by the 2 kilometre cross country run. This list of accepted entries in 1975 gives an idea of the wide national and even international appeal of the event.

Swiss Academic Ski Club of Zurich

Cairngorm Ski Club	Dunfermline College Ski Club
Durham University	Edinburgh University Ski Club
Glencoe Ski Club	1st Battalion Grenadier Guards
Hatfield Polytechnic	Helensburgh Ski Club
Aberdeen Ski Club	Aberdeen University Ski Club.
Bearsden Ski Club	Bearsden Ladies Ski club
Perth Ski Club	Cranwell Royal Air Force College
Scottish Ski Club Ladies	Birmingham University Modern Pentathlon
Royal Air Force Kinloss	Royal Air Force Leuchars
Royal Air Force Strike Command	Royal Army Ordnance
Royal Bank Ski Club	1st Battalion Royal Scots
4th Royal Tank Regiment	St Andrews University
8th Regiment, Royal Signals	Scottish Infantry Depot
Ski Council of Wales	1st. Batt. Parachute Regiment
Royal Caledonian Curling Club, London Province	

The Pentathlon was always oversubscribed and in the reserve pools, teams included Argyll and Sutherland Highlanders, Ski Club of Great Britain, Dundee Ski Club, Heriot Watt University, Loughborough Colleges Pentathlon Club, Army Physical Training Corps and Merseyside Ski Club.

The patrons, or at least the Chieftains, of the Highland Pentathlon were invariably chosen from the ranks of the distinguished and the famous. 1975 saw Christopher Brasher officiating and he will always be remembered as the pace maker for Roger Bannister's famous sub-four minute mile in 1954 and an Olympic Gold Medal winner in the 3000 metre steeplechase at the 1956

Melbourne Games. Also taking part and overseeing the ceremonies in other years were John Ridgway the Atlantic rower, Brendan Foster, David Wilkie the swimmer, Chris Brasher, Menzies (Ming) Campbell and the Duke of Argyll.

Held by tradition at the end of the ski season in late April, there was only one year, 1981, when the skiing leg of the Pentathlon could not be held because of the end of season snow shortage. On that occasion canoeing was substituted and a one kilometre sprint course was set on Loch Morlich. The military provided the Pentathlon Technical Advisor and a statistics unit while I became involved as the Technical Delegate for the skiing leg of the competition. As for the all important sponsorship, John Player took on the considerable costs involved in giving hospitality and accommodation to 130 athletes and officials.

After 10 years the sponsorship was taken over by William McEwan (equally popular). The honours went round many individuals and teams involved. As a footnote I should record that the Scottish Ski Club, men and ladies, featured in the winners lists as did the Bearsden Club, the Cairngorm Club and, the Aberdeen Club won bronze and got into the top six on several occasions.

Aberdeen Club team with John Ridgeway the Atlantic rower

Glenmore Lodge

Clive Freshwater joined the professional staff at the lodge in 1959 and I met him that year when I did two weeks at Easter as a voluntary instructor. Later, our paths crossed over many years on Cairngorm and at the end of ski seasons we had a traditional annual game of golf on courses in the Spey Valley. I admired the man's single mindedness in leaving his safe job at Glenmore Lodge after ten years, to branch out and realise his personal dream by creating his own company, from scratch and against huge odds.

The Lodge in those years was offering training courses for the public, for youth leaders and teachers. I volunteered as an odd-job instructor in the days before strict regulation and certification became necessary to allow anyone to lead groups into the mountains. My membership of the Cairngorm Mountaineering Club and my time with mountain rescue was sufficient for me to be accepted. I took small groups up onto the Ben Macdhui plateau and the surrounding hills, doing a little snow and ice climbing, some instruction on snow shelter building, and mountain navigation.

Just once or twice I had to take very small groups of skiing beginners on to the lower slopes of Cairngorm where I proved to be only marginally more skilled than my class. Thank goodness Frith Finlayson wasn't watching. Marriage, mortgage and parenthood followed those years but I remembered them well. I met several of the staff of the Lodge including Alec Drysdale, the principal and Jack Thomson a senior instructor. Plumb Worrel and Ben Humble were there in my time and of course, Clive Freshwater.

I wrote this article for the Scottish Field in 1987 simply because I thought the man was right in his struggles to set up his own business and the authorities and vested interests were out of order.

Freshwater On The Spey   *Scottish Field* 1987

Clive Freshwater will be remembered as the man who won the most famous battle of the Spey ... a legal battle, simply stated as "canoeing versus salmon fishing". The fight was not of Freshwater's making. In fact he was singled out in the beginning to be a sacrificial lamb. The Trustees of the Knockando Estate issued a writ against Clive's Cairngorm Canoe, Sailing and Ski School which operated from Loch Insh near Aviemore. They sought to prevent him from taking small groups of canoeists down the river water which passed through the estate, because, they maintained, he was interfering with the salmon.

Fishing rights are jealously protected and for many river owners, can be lucrative. I thought then and think now, "how on earth can someone own a river?" The canoe was seen as a threat to these historical interests, but even today there is little proof of economic loss to the traditional sports, following the recreational revolution of the past 20 years. Clive Freshwater became part of the revolution in 1959 when he joined the staff at Glenmore Lodge, the Scottish Sport's Council Outdoor Training Centre near Loch Morlich. He taught skiing, sailing, and mountaineering to teachers and youth leaders. In 1969 he took the big step, leaving salary and security behind. Using a rented village hall and a derelict boat house, he opened for business.

Less than three years later he was served with the writ. The legal action could also have been raised against large national organisations which also used the Spey; for example, the Sports Council itself, Education Authorities and even the Armed Services all used the river. Against his lawyer's advice Clive chose to fight. "I have no quarrel with fishermen," he said, "but the facts are wrong, and it was a matter of principle". Four years later he sat in the House of Lords and listened to Lord Hailsham and Lord Salmon pronounce in his favour. In final judgement it was decided that the case of the Duke of Gordon versus the Grant Family in 1782 had established a public right of navigation on the River Spey. At that time the vessels concerned were rafts of timber, steered by men with crude oars.

That classic legal battle proved to be only an opening skirmish in Freshwater's fight to establish his centre. Subsequently he had to fight his way through a jungle of confusion, red tape and bloody-mindedness. "I spent a third of my time dealing with restrictive legislation administered by various agencies". His Loch Insh Centre began on a plot leased from the Forestry Commission for only three years. Clive had to have safe tenure before he could find financial backing and it was only constant pressure on the Commission that brought an extension of lease to 10 years. Later they give him an option to extend but no possibility to purchase.

Ironically, the Forestry Commission at that very time was selling off parcels of land under the privatisation plans of government.. That knowledge only served to puzzle and irritate Clive Freshwater. When Sir Robin Ives was appointed by Mrs, Thatcher to speed the entire privatisation programme for British industry, Clive wrote and then spoke directly to him. Within five days of stating his case, Clive received a call from the Secretary of State for Scotland, to say that the Forestry Commission had been instructed to sell the eight acres of leased land and to offer him further adjoining land.

The centre was able to grow. An impressive stone and timber Boat House and Restaurant was built by the shore of the Loch and the recreational centre flourished. But, such is the complexity of land tenure, the conflict of interest, lack of national planning and too many quangos, further problems lay ahead. The Nature Conservancy Council slapped a "Site of Special Scientific Interest" on parts of Freshwater's land, stating that it contained a unique stand of mature poplar trees. Shortly before that restricting order was placed, Clive had thinned out some of the trees, acting on the advice of a professional forester who described the trees as "weeds". There was more to come, for the N.C.C. and the R.S.P.B wanted to take ownership of the solum or bed of Loch Insh which would have given them the right to withdraw boating rights by declaring the 700 acres of the loch, a S.S.S.I. Freshwater will survive but the list of obstacles he has to overcome grows longer each year.

Footnote 2010:

Freshwater did survive and has built an award winning business in the Spey Valley, given Royal approval when Princess Anne formally opened the enlarged Loch Insh Watersports, Boathouse Restaurant and Insh Ski Lodges just a few years ago. He has become a major employer in the Spey Valley and combined with his own growing business he was also Chairman of BASI for 11 or more years. The British Association of Ski Instructors based in Grantown on Spey is now an internationally recognised professional body with 5,000 members worldwide.

Throughout this book I have referred to BASI Grade 1 instructors as being the top qualification of three grades of instructor. To my astonishment, I now

Clive Freshwater

find that the present managing committee have reversed the grading system so that the top instructors are now Grade 3 and the lowest, Grade 1. There is little logic in that change and there are growls of discontent from the ski teaching fraternity and I would not be at all surprised if the many older instructors cause committee minds to be changed and the system reverts to Grade 1 for the top teachers. It sounds as if that was change for change's sake. To most folk, top grade means Grade 1 ... followed by, second class and third class.

The Ptarmigan Flies Again

On an historical note, literally thousands of Scots will remember the Ptarmigan Cafe which sat beside the chairlift top station at 400ft below the summit of Cairngorm. It provided essential shelter and sustenance for the thousands who skied in both the Coire na Ciste and on the White Lady. When the Cairngorm mountain railway was built in 2001 the old welcome shelter and café was demolished to make way for the new restaurant and viewing station. The curved laminated timber frames went into storage for several years only to be rediscovered by Clive Freshwater. The iconic domed building has been re-furbished and erected by the side of the Loch Insh Boathouse and Lodges where it now serves as the sports clothing and equipment shop. It was such a welcome refuge in its day and when the blizzards raged it could accommodate 250 or more skiers packed in like sardines, steaming gently together while fighting for a hot coffee. Happy memories!

The Ptarmigan rebuilt at Loch Insh

Chapter 11

Sir Arnold Lunn

The K Club

I first became aware of the grand old man of British ski sport in 1969 when he was living out his long life in his favourite home, his "Eagles Nest". At the time he was into his 80s and living above the traditional old village of Murren in Switzerland with its incredible views across the deep valley to both the Jungfrau and the Eiger. He was still skiing, very gently and slowly but with obvious pleasure. He had been knighted in 1952 for services to British skiing and Anglo-Swiss relations.

It was only when I skied at Murren and worked with the Kandahar Ski Club that I realised that Murren was indeed the cradle of the modern sport. The British/English had adopted the Swiss Wengen/Murren region from early in the last century and several British ski clubs were founded and based in Switzerland. Sir Arnold had been a founder of the Alpine Ski Club in 1908 and also the Kandahar Club based in Murren in 1924. An energetic pioneer alpinist and skier he was a prodigious writer, a romantic about "the mountains" and a historian with amazing recall.

He was credited with inventing and running the first ever slalom races in Murren, and devising the international rules for slalom still used today, in essence. He was the author of many books about alpine mountaineering and skiing in the late 19th century and early 20th. century and a member of the Lunn dynasty which pioneered early tourist holidays to the European Alps. The family still has links in that market.

The young Arnold turned to the politics of skiing after a serious climbing accident in 1909 which limited his skiing from then on. As an organiser, he developed a passion for downhill skiing and he fronted a campaign for the recognition of downhill racing as opposed to the Nordic forms.

With the re-birth of the Olympic Games in 1896, all world sportsmen and women were given a chance to become supreme champions. The protagonists for Nordic and Alpine skiing were left out in the cold, for the movement to re-establish the Olympic movement believed at first that only traditional summer sports should feature. Lunn helped to cut through the conflict between the Nordic style of skiing and the European modernisers who wanted to promote downhill and slalom in the Swiss and the Austrian Alps and for those sports to become Olympic sports.

I had referred to one of Arnold Lunn's books entitled, "Mountain Jubilee" published in 1943. Lunn was exiled from his home in Switzerland by the proximity of the Nazis and was on board ship to America when he wrote the preface for the book. He spoke of the "Golden Age of British Skiing" and he really was a prime influence in the shaping of the world sport of skiing … over 100 years ago. The development surge in Scotland in the second half of last century was very different as I have tried to describe, for it was the people's sport.

Mount Everest

Lunn had a way with words and he was always well aware that he was a pioneer, a trail blazer for the development of Alpine Skiing as we know it today. He invented rules for the new sport, he lobbied and argued and had his way in many confrontations. He was an amazing man in so many ways. In his book Mountain Jubilee he talked endlessly of the lure of the mountains, the challenges, the romance and the camaraderie among those who took part. He talked also of Andrew Irvine, the climbing partner of George Leigh Mallory, the two who died on Mount Everest in 1924.

Irvine was an honorary member of the Kandahar Club and had just learned to ski over the Christmas period in Murren. In writing to Lunn at that time he said, "I will look back on Christmas 1923 as the day when to all intents and purposes I was born. I don't think anybody has ever lived until they have been on skis". Arnold Lunn described Irvine as being one of the most remarkable beginners he had ever seen, "After just three weeks on skis in the middle of January he left Murren to cross the Oberland glaciers. I never saw him again".

The Alpine Club sent out the British Everest Expedition in 1924 with very high hopes of success. It was a club for gentlemen … who happened to climb and Mallory was the darling of the establishment. Irvine's inclusion was a last minute decision and despite his lack of high altitude experience he was chosen at the last minute by Mallory for the last push to the summit.

The two mountaineers died on Everest and while one body has been located, we will never know if one or both reached the summit. We like to think that they did.

To quote Sir Arnold again: *"The English (and the Scots) have invented more than a fair share of the world's best games, and have usually ended up by being soundly beaten by their pupils. The story of downhill racing is no exception to the rule. But at least we who have sponsored the Downhill and invented the Slalom had the fun of racing when racing was young. There is no Alpine valley which was not potentially capable of producing ten times as many first class racers as the Ski Club of Great Britain. In the Alps, skiing is the people's sport. British skiing is the sport of that privileged class which can afford the time and the money for a winter holiday".*

Required Reading

In his book, "The Making of Modern Britain", published in 2009, Andrew Marr devoted a section to Arnold Lunn and the period from the beginning of the 20th century until the end of World War Two. He referred to him as the one Englishman whose contribution was so huge, that he is still remembered throughout the skiing world. By the mid 1920's his rules for downhill and slalom skiing had been internationally accepted, and downhill skiing was an Olympic sport. Through the 1920's and 30's , British skiers were rivalled only by the Swiss for speed and technique, and brought to Switzerland the hard partying, mildly glamorous atmosphere the great Swiss resorts enjoyed between the wars. The Lunn's golden age would only end with the rise of fascism and the war.

I found another mine of information in the book by Roland Huntford published in 2008. Take this for example; in 1843 the local newspaper in the North Norwegian port of Tromso, carried this advertisement.

INVITATION TO A RACE ON SKIS   February. 1843

On Tuesday afternoon of Tuesday the 21st inst,. Weather and snow conditions permitting, a few people propose to test the speed of their ski and the extent of their powers in a race from the Town Hall to the well of Herr Ebertoft's farm on the other side of the island and back again to the starting point. All who are interested in a true Norwegian sport are invited to take part.

This was the first ever published announcement of a ski race. And, later when the results were published, it was the very first known recorded press coverage of ski racing in the world; and it hit the front pages … in Norway. As a freelance journalist and reporter on ski sport in Scotland in the last half century, I was impressed by the meticulous research carried out by Huntford for his book, "Two Planks and a Passion. The Dramatic History of Skiing".

Andrew Marr's piece about the Lunn dynasty entitled "Downhill all the Way" tells the story of how British society changed in the years between the death of Queen Victoria in 1901 and the end of the Second World War in 1945. Marr the political journalist and media commentator and a Scot from Glasgow, sketched out how the British had helped in opening up Europe by leading the way to foreign travel and exciting new sports including Alpine skiing.

Whisky Courage

My only meeting with Sir Arnold in Murren in 1969 was when our team of Scottish race organisers were invited to help run the Kandahar Martini

International. I have talked about his place in the history of British and World skiing in the first half of the twentieth century. He was a giant in his time and his writings influenced me over the years. When invited to meet him and enjoy his hospitality, the most important part for me was studying his many large photograph albums which chronicled seventy of his active years when he influenced the early development of ski sport in Europe. He called those years between the two world wars, the "Golden Years of British Skiing"

At the meeting, I found the courage to suggest that Scottish skiers would soon emerge as a major force in the British Ski Teams. He was silent for a moment but then dismissed my suggestion abruptly. But he did top up my whisky glass. It was an embarrassing moment but, I have just come across a photograph of Sir Arnold taken at the British Alpine Junior Championships held in Andermatt in 1973, just four years after my meeting and shortly before his death. He is seen with eight junior racers, all holding winners cups. Seven of the eight were Scots and they were: Lisi Fuchs, Douglas MacDonald, Roddy Langmuir, Ian Watt, Alistair Scobbie, Duncan Riley and Nicholas Ayles. I remember them all for they were prominent at the many Scottish Junior race events I helped to organise. Where are they all now I wonder? Perhaps my prophesy in 1969 had some credence after all and certainly, the post-war half century proved to be Scotland's Golden Skiing Years.

Dipping again into those books, I find that political battles broke out when the first Modern Olympic Games started in 1896. These summer games took place in Greece in honour of the first games held 1500 years before. Meanwhile, the Scandinavian lobby had dreams of making Nordic skiing an international sport at Olympic level. At that time Norway and Sweden were joined together under one king, having been united by the Congress of Vienna in 1814, but, they lived together in uneasy partnership. The Norwegians longed for independence, and when it was achieved, no one was surprised. On 7th June 1905, Norway simply declared that Oscar II King of Sweden, was no longer King of Norway, and the unsatisfactory union was dissolved while the new King Haakon took the throne of Norway. In 1949 the World Rover Scout Moot look place at Lom in the Norwegion mountains and Crown Prince Olav of Norway was our patron, shaking hands with our scruffy Rover Scout Crew from Aberdeen.

But, skirmishing continued between the two countries over their individual attitudes to their joint national sport ... Nordic style skiing. They both wanted their particular brands of the sport to become the models for the increasingly popular world sport. In the European Alps, downhill skiing had crept in, as a recreation, rather than as a practical skill as in Scandinavia. It followed in the footsteps of the 19th century Alpinists who had systematically conquered all the principal mountains in Europe. The British were there of course as major players, as travellers, early tourists, explorers and climbers. My battered copy of Edward Whimper's "Scrambles in the Alps", has pride of place on my book shelves today. First published in1871, it chronicled his early climbing years from 1860-1869, including the first ascent of the Matterhorn from the Italian side, in which four of his colleagues were so tragically killed.

The James Bond Episode

The Kandahar Martini International Races in Murren in 1969 also coincided with the filming of "On Her Majesty's Secret Service", the new Bond film in the series. The Scottish race officials, having helped to run the race event, had a couple of days of free time, before flying back home. We had intended to grab as much of the time left, skiing on the slopes below the Schilthorn mountain, but an intriguing opportunity arose which topped off an amazing trip to the Swiss Alps. We had been aware that film crews were working in and around the area and we had witnessed some of the filming for the "Bob Sleigh" episode, taking place on nearby slopes.

On our last day of free skiing before going home, our early breakfast was interrupted by a knock on the door of our chalet and it was a recruiter for the film company. He needed some 20 film extras for that day and would we be interested? The fee was to be £5. He was recruiting around the village for anyone who had ski clothing and skis. Initially, we as a group said no, a day's skiing was our first priority and £5 was not a sufficient temptation, so at first we turned him down.

Within minutes we had reassessed the situation and changed our minds. A mad dash followed as we scoured the village to catch up with him and to enlist. We were required to report at 11am, to the top of the Schilthorn, at 9,652ft., which is topped by an amazing revolving restaurant overlooking the Jungfrau and Eiger peaks. After two hours of free skiing we reported as required and were taken down to the basement area to be kitted out with uniforms and guns. Exciting stuff. We were to become actors in an action movie! Not just any action movie but a James Bond movie!

There were two groups of skiers to be filmed as extras that day, the goodies and the baddies and the selection for who played which part, depended on the colour of one's ski pants. My pants were black and so I was given a stylish orange ski jacket and a rather fetching astrakhan hat and a tommy gun. We were all elated by the prospect of playing war games on top of a big mountain, in Switzerland, on snow and with very realistic guns. It's a boy thing, but I was to be disappointed!

The James Bond Warriors

Leading Men

The Director briefed us and placed us in position in and around the revolving mountaintop restaurant and, again I drew a short straw. But first, I should sketch out the plot for the day's filming. The evil baddies were based on the top of the mountain and the goodies were being flown in by helicopters to attack and destroy their citadel, and to free James Bond from their clutches. Three helicopters containing the goodies, were already in the air with a filming helicopter above them, recording the action from above

My dreams of stardom then began to fade. The filming director placed me face down, bloodied and contorted, in the snow outside the citadel. I was to remain dead while all the action took place above me. There were three takes for that one shot, for some technical reason and all the while I was required to remain, face down in cold snow and to be definitely dead. I did cheat and turned over, merely to be blinded by the helicopter snow downdraft.

To add to my disappointment that day, I was then told that Sean Connery was not the hero in the film. It was some unknown Australian actor called George Lazenby who played the part, disappointingly, according to the critics, and then disappeared into anonymity. My acting career also ended at that point but further disappointment was still to come. Others in our team of race officials were the good guys and dressed accordingly. Instead of being paid off after shooting finished on top of the Shilthorn, four of them were asked to do some overtime with extra pay.

We bad and dead men, received our £5 pay packets and skied back to our chalet. They on the other hand, were loaded into the helicopters and had to fly around the face of the Eiger and the Jungfrau several times for a further 30 minutes just as the sun was setting. The result was some of the most dramatic mountain cinematography imaginable and, to be a witness and a film extra taking part must have been exciting. I missed all that and simply became a very dead bit player.

When I received free tickets to take my family to see the film's premier in Aberdeen later that year, the only comment I had from my first son, then aged seven was, "Is that you Dad? Why are you dead? ". The only point in the film that sparked some excitement for him came at the bit where other baddies were chasing James Bond on skis and he tricked them into falling beneath the whirring blades of a huge snow cutter and blower. It was a gloriously gory bit of filming with chunks of broken skis, red meat and ski boots being spewed out by the revolving blades. My part in that James Bond film was so insignificant that not even my own children were impressed and I was never able to dine out on the story.

Chapter 12

Scribbler

Freelance

Reporting ski competition led to travel writing, as companies began to include me on press trips to ski and also to write about summer resorts. I met the late Erna Low several times when she invited me to join her travel groups and I think I became her token Scottish journalist. Later, I represented her company at national Ski Shows in London and Birmingham and travelled with her to the Alps, Sicily and the Alpe Adria region encompassing Yugoslavia and Austria.

Erna's own story was fascinating, for she first came to Britain in the early 1930's as a student and to help pay for her studies she began to take guided ski parties to Austria, her homeland. The Second War halted that, but she took British nationality, changed her name from Lowe to Low and built up her famous travel company, becoming a big name by 1980, in the travel consultancy world. Erna was a sportswoman in her youth, winning the Austrian javelin championship and, she excelled at skiing and tennis.

Peter Emslie the late solicitor from Banchory and I were in effect, the first press officers for Scottish skiing, reporting for several Scottish newspapers. He later took on a more official role with the SNSC, while I diversified into more general feature writing. We were both heavily involved with organising club and national racing at that time and we both had seats on the Scottish National Ski Council Executive Committee. I later retired as a Vice President from the Council. It was time for new blood.

In the early 1960s the Scottish press was barely aware of what was happening and apart from infrequent reports about some mountain developments, no attempts were made to make even brief mention of national competitions or the rapid growth of the sport. Sections of the English national press were perhaps unaware that skiing had become such a popular sport north of the border. Some cynics even suggested that Fleet Street could barely point to where Scotland was on a map.

As popularity of the sport, grew, there were more opportunities to provide competition results to newspapers across Britain. The Yorkshire Post was interested, for Martin and Graham Bell were the top British skiers for a decade or more and their parents had settled in Yorkshire to run an outdoor centre with a ski slope. The Newcastle Journal took some feature material and eventually, I was in the position to supply races results to around 12 newspapers including the Express, Mail, Mirror,

Eddie the Eagle

Times, Telegraph, Guardian and occasionally I was asked to provide feature articles. The Today newspaper asked me for 1000 words about Eddie the Eagle which I supplied after frantic research. He was a figure of fun in some quarters, frowned on by the London skiing establishment for cheapening the image of the sport by coming last in the Olympics. I thought he was a brave lad. Not many skiers would attempt to jump off into space as he did.

The paper used my piece in its entirety and paid me handsomely. My only complaint was that my article appeared under the name of a staff journalist. I assumed that he was also well paid and that that kind of double accounting led to the eventual financial demise of that paper. The newspaper industry was in turmoil as the strangle hold of the unions was being

About to fly

loosened. The Today paper was floated in 1986 by Eddy Shah, sold within months to Tiny Rowlands and it folded in 1995.

I also became a regular contributor to the Scottish Field, The Aberdeen Leopard magazine, two or three ski magazines including the American Ski magazine which was fascinated to hear about Scottish skiing. I took my own photographs to accompany my copy and many appear in this book. Occasional work followed from Grampian Television and BBC, mainly on skiing topics. It was all fun and it allowed me to indulge in my own passion for the mountains. Grampian Television was one of the first companies to take a big interest in the sport and for many years was a major sponsor. It began in 1962 when they sent cameras to cover the Bon Accord Giant slalom run by the Highland Ski Club on Cairngorm. By 1963, the race meeting became the Grampian Television Giant Slalom event and later, the North of Scotland Senior Championships with both Giant Slalom and Slalom events organised by the Aberdeen club.

The Chief Executive, Mr. Ward Thomas, was a supreme enthusiast and despite cancellation of the first race because of severe weather, he deployed his team of cameras and technicians the following week, in the Corrie na Ciste. This was long before the first lifts were built in the Ciste and it was a tough climb and hard work for everyone. Karl Fuchs built a very long open course with only fourteen gates which was described by David Banks of Perth, a past Scottish Champion as "one long schuss". The weather for filming was good and the following television sports programme became the first of its kind in Scotland. Grampian Television as I said, continued to be a major sponsor for several years and, their participation prompted other major sponsors to give their support.

Chapter 13

Global Warming

Or Ice Age ?

In Scotland we are all too aware of the effects of climate change and the apparent evidence seems to be growing. Snow falls are now intermittent and the existing ski centres no longer have predictable seasons and, there has been a big reduction in skiing numbers at Scotland's five centres in recent years. While the centres still open for business as soon as snow does fall, the crowds flock in. However the long term future may seem to be grey and perhaps even bleak. Unless that is, global warming is short lived and is quickly followed by a mini ice age. BUT, stranger things have happened!

In just recent times, conflicting information about climate change forecasts are being announced. World wind and weather patterns, typhoons, severe flooding across the world are changing the picture. In relation to Scottish skiing conditions in just two years, 2010 and 2011, something quite dramatic has happened. It was not forecast, but now our "experts" reveal that we can expect similar winter changes for the next decade.

The historians confirm that little ice ages have occurred over many centuries and in recent years there has been much more scientific information gathered about them. The mini freezes brought colder winters to much of the northern hemisphere with disastrous consequences for some countries. In the mid 17th. century the River Thames froze over and people skated and walked across and even held "frost fairs" when goods were sold, music played and people danced on the ice. In some years the Baltic froze over, when horses and men were able to cross to Sweden from Poland.

Looking at the available records from the 16th to the mid 19th centuries it seems that there were three episodes of very cold periods, beginning around 1650, again about 1770 and then around 1850, each separated by warmer periods. Now, that suggests that about every century or so, Europe suffered from colder winters. The fact is that these chilly episodes were followed by warming periods, when our northern hemisphere countries enjoyed good crops, luscious fruits, a good life and, populations increased. When the severe winters returned, crops failed to mature, starvation weakened people and animals and pestilence followed.

Melting Glaciers

Who can we believe? There is so much conflicting information or misinformation flying about, that it really is confusing. We were told that the Himalayan glaciers would all melt by 2035 but, that prediction has now been scaled down, dramatically. We were also told that the melting of the polar ice caps will raise sea levels around the world.

Strangely, there is hard existing evidence that the land mass of Scotland is actually rising out of the sea, by measurable amounts each decade, after having been pushed down by the enormous weight of ice during the last Ice Age. Have you ever sailed down the west coast of the island of Jura? If you have, you will have seen the raised stone and pebble beaches lying 150 feet above today's sea level. It is an astonishing sight and great food for thought.

Weather ... Will it or Won't it?

Few can deny that something is happening. But, what is? What does the future hold? Do we mothball our skiing facilities in the hopes that a mini ice age could come to pass sometime soon, or do we just resign ourselves to the fact that it was great while it lasted and move on to take up other exciting "new" sports like mountain biking, paragliding, bungee jumping or bingo?

While we are chatting about the improbable, the unlikely and the ridiculous, I am reminded that not so long ago Ed Milliband, then Energy and Climate Change Secretary in the Brown Government, made a new appointment. A Cambridge academic called Professor David MacKay from the illustrious Cavendish Laboratory was recruited as a new government advisor on climate change. These appointments of advisors are made from time to time as governments seek to recruit specialist brains into the think tanks in the corridors of power. Some of these recruits quickly fade back into obscurity, others burned brightly for a spell before retiring to the House of Lords while many can't stand the heat in the kitchen and so just resign discreetly and go back to their ivory towers.

MacKay became a bright star in 2009 when he published his book, "Sustainable Energy ... Without Hot Air". It quickly became a best seller despite the title, simply because he used the unlikely combination of wit and mathematics to dismiss the many assumptions we all have about the topic and to dismiss the hogwash which he describes as "greenwash".

Vital Ingredient

MacKay's book caught my eye because he sketched out a role for Scotland's biggest renewable resources, water and wind. We have plenty of both and we already produce some 12% of our power from water turbines. I always did like the thought that snow, once skied upon, melts and runs down the burns and streams to become the vital ingredient in the production of whisky. Then to fill the dams which generate power which would heat the water for my bath where I would be relaxing after a good day on the snow, while enjoying a large glass of whisky. That to my mind would be the perfect way to recycle everything. But back to reality.

What Global Warming ?

In the new millennium, the prophets of doom were gathering together to confuse us even more and, record high temperatures across Britain even gave them more credence. Then came 2009/10 and the coldest winter in over twenty or thirty years in Scotland … some said even longer. The temperature plummeted to well below freezing and stayed low as heavy snow falls caused further chaos for weeks on end. Europe too, had the deep freeze and having skied in Val d'Isere in France that same winter, we spent a week enjoying some of the very cold but best of snow conditions. The day time temperatures were extremely low, -20 degrees centigrade and with the wind chill factor, that is cold! Definitely "Long John weather"

We even kept an eye on each other's noses and cheeks for little tell-tale white patches, just in case. Today, I still have a slight scar tissue blemish on the tip of one ear, from frost bite gained in Switzerland while gate watching at a British Championships race at Sils in the Engedine Valley near St. Moritz. The British Team Manager at the Championships was Alistair Scobbie from Alloa and he was flown home prematurely because of frost bitten toes. Even the sponsor, Sir John Ritblat had a frost bite scare. I am quite proud of that honourable little scar on my ear and, I still have all my toes.

The recent very cold seasons raised doubts in many people's minds and global warming predictions suddenly became confused, together with most of the population. Further doubts were sown in the public mind as learned climatologists were accused of using selective research results to strengthen their own particular research programmes. The British predilection for opening a conversation with comments about the weather … *"nasty day"* or *"fine day"* was replaced in the icy winters, by a quizzical, *"what about this global warming then?"*.

In Highland Perthshire we had minus 17 degrees centigrade several times over many weeks and frequent heavy falls of snow. This created one of the most memorable ski seasons for many years with full car parks and bustling crowds even in mid-week. Glencoe even declared at one point that it just had the biggest snow fall in the whole world! By and large the five ski centres rose to the challenges of finding extra staff at short notice. Some complaints of course

Massive snow drifts on the Cairngorm ski road 1970s

were heard, as ticket offices and ski hire services were swamped. Cairngorm in particular, came under heavy criticism as it was unable to open the ski road for many days because of massive falls of drifting snow. Many potential customers fretted down in the Spey Valley ... or, diverted to Lecht or Glenshee.

It transpired that the chairlift company had sold off the heavy snow clearing machines designed for such extreme snowfalls, presumably because they were being used less in recent times and, were worth a lot of money. Cairngorm was in serious debt following the building of the 15 million pound funicular railway in 2001 and had already decommissioned the chairs and tows in the Corrie na Ciste. The finances at Cairngorm had always been difficult and became more so, as other agencies became involved. It would seem that too many cooks are still attempting to manage the whole Cairngorm area, unsuccessfully today.

The Cairngorm Chairlift Company did dip a toe into the money lending market in 1984. In Bob Clyde's day, they entered into an agreement with the

Royal Bank of Scotland's corporate lending arm, National, Commercial and Glynn's, who agreed to lend £800,000 to the Cairngorm Chairlift Company, the non-profit making venture. The money was to be used to complete the biggest investment ever to that point … the £1.25 million Day Lodge which was to provide shelter, food, shopping and ski hire facilities. The unfinished shell of the huge building had been lying unfinished for two years and had been funded originally by the Highlands and Islands Development Board with its 30% grant. After £450,000 had been spent on foundations and steel work, the cash ran out. At the time it was described as the most unusual bank lending deal ever struck in Scotland.

The obvious problem was that the company's fortunes each year were totally dependent on the weather. The seesaw nature of the business was illustrated by the figures revealed at the time.

1980-81 on a turnover of £732,000, a loss of £174,000
1981-82 on a turnover of £887,500, a loss of £54,000
1982-83 on a turnover of £1.2 million, a record profit of £188,000

The skeleton of the unfinished Cairngorm Day Lodge

I never did follow through the story of Cairngorm finances but I did know that Bob Clyde wanted to install snow making machines as soon as the debt was paid off. The debts increased and there were no snow makers on the hill.

Quango Questions

Still in 2010, to sell off the principal machines essential to keeping the ski road and therefore the entire Cairngorm business open, was indeed careless, if not culpable. Now that we have the Cairngorm National Park with the Cairngorm ski centre in the Park, many of us are confused about who actually does what. For instance, when I skied Cairngorm at Easter 2010 the ticket system did not appear to be working. My family started off by finding their feet on the beginners slope before taking the Carpark/Day Lodge T bar tow to the Cas Tow and up that tow. No one asked to see a pass or tickets all day and we skied much of the time in that area because the younger ones were not ready for the upper slopes. I cannot recall that ever happening in the past. Were they short of staff? Whose job was it to issue and check tickets? Someone was badly organised. How much income did they miss that day while Cairngorm was heavily in the red? There were five in our family group and every little would have helped. Worth a bob or two!

Scottish Review

To underline my personal thoughts, I quote the following:
"... *running Britain requires a cabinet committee of 23; running the Cairngorm National Park Authority requires the same number. Of the UK Westminster cabinet members, 23 are paid. But on Cairngorm, everybody's paid. Although in the financial year 2008-09 the authority claimed to have 23 members, it succeeded in handing out fees and expenses to 27, because of mid-year changes of appointments.*

This is not bad work if you can get it. Lots do. The part-time chairman was on £20,441 plus expenses of £11,025. The others were paid up to £10,221 for attending meetings. The total bill for committee members in 2008-09, the year of the great financial crash … was £195,195 [up from £177,164 the previous year] with another £29,084 being paid in expenses. No one, but no one, served on the Cairngorm National Park Authority for the love of it …"

That was penned by Kenneth Roy in the Scottish Review of June 2010. Labelling this, *"a colossal waste of public money",* he called for the reduction of the Board of the Cairngorm National Park Association from 23 to six. Now, I know little about the Cairngorm National Park Authority and indeed about those who now manage Cairngorm Mountain. How are they interlinked? However, I might just get on the internet and find out a bit more about them and their functions for I always felt that I have a vested interest in the Cairngorm developments.

I do have a long memory, and in 1958 when in Jimmy Ross's wee pub and hotel, the Rowanlee, in Carrbridge, there was a campaign to raise funds to push a road up to the big mountain, to the foot of Corrie Cas. Having climbed up to the Cas and Jean's Hut over several years, I knew every boulder on the track and the thought of actually being able to drive up there, was very attractive indeed. At that point I hadn't envisaged that there might eventually be chairlifts and ski tows to get to the top of Cairngorm, these followed later.

In a moment of madness I put a fiver in the box on the bar to swell the fund. That was one quarter of my weekly wage at the time. So yes! I was in at the very beginning of it all and so, yes, I do have a vested interest. Today, the decommissioning of several lifts and tows in the Coire na Ciste have ruffled many feathers and I find there is a strong movement to *"Save the Ciste".* I clicked on that and found an articulate movement against the shutdown of ski facilities. The management is not even maintaining and mothballing the facilities; rusting cables and dereliction are sadly obvious. The opening statement by this movement kicks off by saying, *"While being acutely aware of the many competing needs for limited funding on Cairngorm Mountain it is our view that the reinstatement of the Coire na Ciste chairlifts and the provision of basic facilities at the Ciste carpark should be of utmost priority".*

Much of what I read in the detailed papers produced by the campaign organisers make sense and added to my gut feeling that something is not right on our Cairngorm Mountain. Is Cairngorm run by a quango? Subsequently I came upon the horror story about the so called bus service laid on to shuttle skiers back from the foot of the Corrie na Ciste in 2010, which was in superb condition but had no lifts. The local bus company hired to do the job, stopped operating in the middle of the day for one and a half hours leaving skiers stranded. The drivers needed lunch! The Ciste was in great condition and was considered the best ski run on the mountain. But, while the skiers could ski down, there was no way back up, except by the special bus service which was intermittent. It might be a bit of a gamble to re-open mothballed lifts. They were opened in 1974 and sadly have been left without maintenance for too long and are a sad sight today.

To add weight to the argument came news from Westminster in 2010 that almost a third of environmental quangos are to be scrapped leading to questions about the government's green agenda. The Sustainable Development Commission is also losing state funding.

Footnote:
According to my Concise Oxford Dictionary, "Quango" is described thus: *"Chiefly derogatory. A semi-public administrative body outside the civil service but receiving financial support from the government, which make senior appointments to it".* - I rest my case.

Chill Wind

Further to my own thoughts on the subject, a chill was sent through the "quangocracy" in the early days of the coalition government of David Cameron. Francis Maude, a battle hardened conservative member from the days of Margaret Thatcher, had been appointed as Minister of the Cabinet

Office in 2010. From that position he rattled many cages, for his position was an ambiguous, catch-all department and title and he exerted great influence over the entire government. Early in that job he was asked to list which of the hundreds of quangos, agencies and non-departmental bodies he was *"assessing on their suitability of purpose and cost-effectiveness"* or in other words, sizing up for the butcher's block.

Instead of providing a list, Mr Maude replied simply: *"all of them".* Colleagues had long considered him as being very effective and sometimes ruthlessly so. Time will tell if he, or a Holyrood counterpart will study the situation in Scotland and in particular the sad story and poor management evident at Cairngorm National Park and Mountain Resort ... and elsewhere.

Chapter 14

Alpine Heights

Mountain Love Affairs

Having had a taste of snow in the Alps, I wanted to see the big mountains in summer. The Aosda Valley in particular excited me and having skied in Cervinia, just beneath the Matterhorn, that classic mountain, it became almost an obsession. Nothing ventured, nothing gained. I wrote to the Italian Tourist Office saying I wished to do a piece about the Aosta Region and could they accommodate me in a press trip. I then joined a group of N American journalists for a week of serious walking in the Grande Paradiso National Park, the Val Tournance and Monte Rosa areas. Later, I presented myself at the Cervinia Bureau des Guides.

There, I was allocated a guide and told to join him early the next morning. Gino Peron was a weathered guide nearing his sixties as I was and who spoke no English and only a quaint mountain patois. This meant that our conversations were limited. He took me to climb one of the finest looking rock peaks in the district as a sort of test run of my competence before he took me to the Matterhorn. The Punta di Cian [or Chinese Peak] at 3320mts. was recognisable by its turreted ridges, one of which provided the most sought-after rock climb in the whole of the Valpelline South-Valtournanche crest area.

That was unforgettable and took me back some thirty years to hair-raising climbs in Raeburns Gully on Lochnagar, scrambles on the cliffs of the Coire Sputan Dearg on Ben Macdhui and the many times on the Cuillins of Skye; the Inaccessible Pinnacle on Sgurr Dearg and the Cioch direct route came sharply to mind.

It was a joy to climb with the grizzled old guide when conversation was barely possible or indeed necessary. That was a 36 hour expedition which meant spending one night in the Refuge Rivolta which was ultra basic, but good, apart for the strong smell of stale urine at the back of the wee hut. Two days later came the Monte Cervino, the Matterhorn.

I wrote up that experience for High Mountain magazine and contrasted the first day of serious climbing up from the Colle del Leone above Cervinia on the less popular route but superior challenge, compared with the Hornli route on the Swiss side. We overnighted in the J.A. Carrel hut perched at 12,582 feet on the south-west ridge of the Matterhorn and the exposure on both sides was fearsome, literally thousands of feet. The tin and wooden hut was quite simply bolted onto the rock with wires.

High Mountain magazine June 1984:

"… That night spent in the refuge was not a happy one. Perched on the south-west ridge of the peak, the Refuge Carrel was well appointed but the thought which pressed heavily on me was, "what the hell am I doing here?" Instead of being tucked up on my orthopaedic mattress with a heating pad, here I was, folded in musty blankets, fully clothed, still shivering and waiting to climb the last 2000 feet of this fearsome mountain. The wind blew up and everything creaked. A shutter blew open and banged for an hour and then spicules of ice or was it falling stones, began to clatter on the tin roof. I had one final fantasy before slipping into semi-consciousness. "What would I do in the black night, if the roof blew off or if a fire broke out? My vision was of trying to descend the Matterhorn … alone and without boots, braces or spectacles".

It was a bleak and windy dawn and the "tigers" were up and about, their aim to be first onto the rock. That logic had also occurred to me because with several climbers heading for the summit and inevitably dislodging stones, it could be hazardous for those below. In winter, at night the mountain is frozen solid and silent. In summer, the mountain never stops moving. There is always the tinkle and the clatter of falling stone. In fact, when we stop to think about it, the Matterhorn is falling down. My concern was to try to get to the top before it did and I was puzzled why the guides were taking so long to get going. A few guideless climbers had set off at dawn, but the guides, each with a single client made no move. Gino eventually took me aside and pointed to a black and sinister mass of cloud moving rapidly toward us. It began to snow as the storm hit us and my guide said, "OK we go down". No one reached the top that day. The early birds turned back in the face of rapidly worsening conditions and our retreat was wet and cold and crampons were of no comfort. Ice and wet snow confronted us on rock which the day before, had been dry and welcoming.

I did return to the Aosta Valley under my own steam but again, the mountain of my desire was denied me as bad weather stopped all climbing during my short September visits.

My main interests and involvement continued to be in British skiing and competition. I had invitations to act in a press liaison capacity at British Championships held in the Alps where I rubbed shoulders with John Samuel of the Guardian and John Hennessey of the Times. For many years, John Ritblat the Chairman of the British Land Property empire, now Sir John, was the major sponsor at these annual championships. He took a keen interest in the sport and in the national teams that took part. I sat at his dinner table during those weeks in the Alps and met guests he invited to ski with him. At Alpe d'Huez one year, these included the then Minister of Sport, Colin Moynahan and Carol Thatcher. Carol was there as a freelance feature writer, to cover the British Land Alpine Ski Championships and to write about John Ritblat, our host. She proved to be good company at his dinner table.

John Ritblat with Colin Monaghan on the right

Chapter 15

Plastic Revolution

Friction

The prophesy that Scots would dominate in the British Ski Teams and also Olympic Teams, did come true. The "Old Guard", in London however, was focussed only on Alpine trained skiers and on the traditional training camps run by the Kandahar and Downhill Only Clubs based in Switzerland. While acknowledging the early impact these clubs made from as early as 1924, the feeling in the 1970s in Scotland was that our native talent was forging ahead having the facilities to ski more frequently on home snow.

By this time Education Authorities in many areas of Scotland had put skiing on the curriculum for secondary pupils. Those within short commuting distance of a ski centre were able to take pupils skiing on weekly sports days as an alternative to more traditional sports. The ski slopes were empty in mid-week and prices were negotiable. But it was the advent of the "Plastic Slope" that really triggered off the rush to get Scots school pupils onto the slopes … plastic and snow. It was the generosity and vision of one man, Boyd Anderson who funded the first and second phases of the Edinburgh Hillend ski slope which at the time was the largest such facility in Europe.

In the north-east, Aberdeen and Grampian Region had training courses for teachers, bringing in professional instructors and advisers. James C. Hunter, the Director of Physical Education was particularly involved. He pressed for the funds to build the Kaimhill Plastic Slope, gave school teachers opportunities to qualify for the Ski Party Leader qualifications introduced by the Scottish National Ski Council. He led his department from the front and also took these qualifications himself. Some of his staff also went on to take professional qualifications with the British Association of Ski Instructors. He was very active in putting ski sport on the school sports curriculum in the north east of Scotland and the first to set aside funds to purchase ski equipment and transport for that purpose. Years later my own grandchildren benefited from his energetic leadership in putting school skiing on the educational curriculum forty years before.

However, some said he could be a difficult man to deal with, as Aberdeen Ski Club found out. The club was one of the leading clubs in Scotland to get dual slalom racing on artificial slopes on a ski league basis. It began at Hillend in Edinburgh on the quarter mile long plastic slope and then in Glasgow Bearsden and at the Glasgow Ski Centre and wherever slopes were deemed long enough. Not only the larger slopes proved to be suitable for such flood lit ski leagues for the Aberdeen Kaimhill slope could accommodate dual, ten gate courses giving short but fairly fluid slalom runs. Times averaged around 14 seconds for each racer and as one skier finished his or her run, the next team member was started automatically. Such was the clamour from schools, clubs, colleges and universities in Aberdeen that A and B leagues had to be arranged within the first month of starting.

Racing Banned

Despite the huge interest created, the Aberdeen Education Authority advised by James Hunter, decided to ban slalom competition, because of the possibility of excessive wear to the plastic matting. There was huge disappointment at the decision, especially as Mr Hunter was Honorary Vice President of the Aberdeen Ski Club at the time. The club mounted a campaign and took it to the very top.

The Club President and Chairman Dr. John Topps wrote to many local politicians and influential folk while I contacted the main manufacturer of the plastic mats, Dendix, then we contacted the major users of the material around Britain and that included the Edinburgh Hillend slope which was heavily used for competition, including international races. Evidence was gathered which showed that provided the slalom poles were moved frequently and the whole slope was given equal use, there was no evidence of excessive wear. The evidence from Hans Kuwall then Manager at Hillend was very positive. He described how many slalom courses were used each week and how many skiers trained through the sticks.

The Aberdeen Ski Club then tried to by-pass their own Honorary Vice-President, James Hunter, by contacting his political masters in Grampian Region. We were invited to a meeting of the Education Committee and were able to make the club's case and submit evidence. In addition to the written evidence from other ski slope managers around GB, we pointed out that competition was the essence of all sport. We cited the success of racing at other cities and towns in Scotland and in England.

The committee heard our submissions politely and while no formal written permission for slalom racing was given, nothing more was said and the club was able to continue with the slalom leagues, for one more season. It proved to be very popular with many schools, colleges and clubs competing. There were however, strained relations between the club and their Hon. Vice Pres.

Grant Aid

Ironically, a decade before, in 1965, the Aberdeen Ski Club was first to investigate the possibilities of creating an artificial ski slope in the city and indeed we were in discussions with the Scottish Education Department in Edinburgh which was prepared to accept our application for grant aid under the Physical Training and Recreation Act. 1937. The club at that time was also pursuing the possibilities of building a clubhouse and shelter near the Glenshee Ski Centre. The Scottish Education Department then said they could not consider two applications and so, because we already had a substantial shelter hut in the upper Butchart's Corrie in Glenshee, built without grant aid, we went with the plan to build the plastic slope in

Aberdeen. The Education Department approved our plan to utilise slopes near their Kaimhill playing fields at the Bridge of Dee and to use the storage and changing facilities, and leasing arrangements were being discussed.

I then had a long letter from Mr. J.A. Kerr Hunter of the Scottish Council of Physical Recreation who had advised Mr. Boyd Anderson about his huge financial contribution to ski sport by funding the Edinburgh Hillend Plastic Slope. He offered to assist our club in any way, for he was convinced that, *"this is the easiest and best way of teaching youngsters and beginners the basic skills of skiing"*.

Jock Kerr Hunter was already a very well known figure in the SCPR, pioneering and organising sports such as basketball where he helped create the Scottish Association and then by popularising pony trekking and skiing for the Scottish Tourist Board. By 1947 he was arranging the first formal skiing holidays with instruction, in the Spey Valley which increased in popularity over several years, long before any access roads or tows existed. "Jock" was described as, "A Human Dynamo" and I believe his motto was: "Nothing happens unless you make it happen.

Events overtook the hopes and ambitions of Aberdeen Ski Club at that point, when the Scottish Office informed me that, *"The Chancellor of the Exchequer has announced that the Government has decided to put into operation additional measures to strengthen the economy, including a reduction in capital expenditure from public funds. I have accordingly to say that although the department will continue to process your application for grant, it will not be possible until further notice to give permission for work to begin. Another letter will be sent to you in due course".*

Tightening of belts and fiscal crunches were happening even in 1965. We never knew if the Aberdeen Club would ever have had that grant to install the plastic slope or indeed would have been able to operate, maintain and finance such a facility. We thought so at the time for the club and the national sport were very upbeat. The Aberdeen Club even in the late 1950s was contemplating buying property near the snow and surveyed two buildings at Balmoral and Braemar and we eventually leased a cottage in Braemar.

Later, the Bearsden Ski Club showed that one club could do what we could only dream of doing. Within two years the Aberdeen Education Department stepped in and the slope was built at Kaimhill but without a lift in the first years. The club leased weekly sessions on the slope and ran tuition classes for members.

Hillend and Ski Leagues

So successful were the leagues at Edinburgh's Hillend ski slope that numbers had to be restricted in 1987 after 10 years of success. The "adults only" rule came into being to exclude seeded junior racers from its six divisions. It was a painful decision, unpopular in some club circles, but the league had become unwieldy with more than 250 skiers taking part and where the balance between national and recreational competition had been lost. The league involved many clubs from the central belt and one weekend result sheet saw the following winners: The Ski Sport League October 1987: Group 1 Bearsden A team. Group II Bearsden B. Group III Edinburgh Scouts Group IV HMS Cochrane. Group V Glen S.C. Group VI Edinburgh S.C.

Today, belts are being tightened again and the popular Edinburgh Hillend Ski Slope is under serious scrutiny. It may have to be privatised, adjoining land may be sold off and the future is unknown, for Lothian Region cannot continue to finance it.

Chapter 16

Anecdotes and Memories

Mountain Man

David Soutar, summarised the skiing possibilities in the pre-ski-lift days, in one of the very first magazines published by the embryo Aberdeen Ski Club in 1958. David was a founder member, an experienced hill walker and a great club man.

The Undiscovered Beauty of the Nearby

In Scotland, we ski wherever we can find snow and that can lead us to some very odd places indeed. What about the links golf course at Balnagask, overlooking Aberdeen Harbour, or the sloping terraces around Foresterhill Royal Infirmary? The keen enthusiast, who is prepared to carry his skis for a few miles, will find suitable snow on Deeside in November and early December on Ben Avon, Beinn a Bhuird or Carn-an-Tuirc.

It can be mid-December before dependable plans can be made and the Ski Bus can head for the Devil's Elbow, some 68 miles from Aberdeen. The bus may have to stop at Sheann Spittal Bridge, because the road above is seldom ploughed. From there we have the choice of a climb to our club hut on Carn-na-Tuirc where we share the use of the "Scottish" rope tow, or the same distance to the Elbow summit where the Dundee Club operate their highly successful J-bar tow on Meal Odhar.

To the north lies Butchart's Corrie and our own club hut, just completed and

David heather hopping

where we intend to operate our own tractor tow. Just over the shoulder between Cairnwell and Carn Aosda, lies Loch Vrotican and some great cross country skiing. The beginners however, need seldom travel far from the buses and the road where plenty of nursery slopes are found.

When heavy snow means Braemar is as far as we can travel, the fields at Abergeldie, six miles beyond Ballater, offer some wonderful skiing. The two Aberdeen clubs operate tows just below Gaellic Hill whenever possible. Skiing on this low ground snow often continues for four, five or more weeks. As the days lengthen and the high roads open, we move farther afield, back to the Elbow or over to Strathdon and the Aberdeenshire-Banffshire county boundary at the top of the Lecht. It was here that the Club's Ferguson tractor made its debut last winter when it proved Hilas Holbourn's designs were good.

Organised bus runs cease towards the end of April but there is still grand skiing to be had, probably the best of the year, in the high Cairngorms. Corrie

Cas, the venue for the proposed chairlift, has been a famous ski ground for many years and can be approached from Jean's Hut at 2,600 feet. Hopefully, in years to come, we will see access to the Coire na Ciste made easier. Here the winter snows build up to a great depth, being protected from the warming sun by its North-east exposure. The one and a quarter mile run down some 1,500 feet is often available until June

And finally, some grand touring country exists around Aberdeen and one of the finest days enjoyed last season by this writer, was spent on Tyrebagger Hill, skiing on paths through the forestry plantations. Norway could not have offered better!

That was penned nearly sixty years ago but I am sure that there will be other Golden Oldies still out there, who will remember the places David Soutar was describing near Aberdeen. Remember too, that the same information about good skiing slopes near centres of populations was being passed around by word of mouth. Arthur's Seat in Edinburgh has some great meadows for skiing and with wonderful views, but, would skiers be banned today? Even in the 1950s we were barred from using some golf courses because ski tracks could freeze and could cause scorching of the grass. We still had many good evenings after dark and by moon light.

Old Age

When we reach venerable old age and become "octo - geraniums" as one grandchild insists in calling us, we have earned our vested interests, and so one can expect to qualify for concessions such as the bus pass and free television licences. To my joy I found at many Alpine ski centres when one became 73, there was a 50% discount on the ski pass. When I got to 75, joy on joy, I got the entire weekly ski pass, free, just a five Euro charge for insurance. Prices in Val d'Isere are pushing up towards 200 euros for a six day pass, while golden oldies ski free.

One hope still lingered, one final ambition. Would I ever get a discount or even a free ski pass in Scotland? Nothing ventured, nothing gained. I boldly asked at the Cairngorm ticket office. I was greeted by a blank stare from a monosyllabic person behind the glass partition, a sour look and a negative response. I had been tempted to mention that I was a share holder, of sorts, in the whole development but I had no share certificate to flourish. I felt a bit foolish and embarrassed for even asking … silly old buffer. But, someone took pity on me in 2010 when I again attempted to play the age card, this time at Glenshee. Of course, it's not that I am mean by nature you understand, it was all part of the research for this book!

I chose a good-to-be-alive day when the snow cover was complete, the wind was light and the sun shone. Chancing my luck, I took off my bonnet to baldly emphasise my great age and started a conversation with a mature gentleman in the ticket kiosk. My opening gambit was, "I skied these hills long before there were any lifts here and because I am told that am now a very old man, is there any chance of a concessionary ticket?". While saying my piece, I took out my wallet preparing to pay. My hand was gently pushed aside and a day ticket was slipped into it.

It transpired the gentleman had skied in the 1960s and he and I had probably rubbed shoulders or crossed skis, in the years when the Abergeldie slopes near Balmoral on Deeside were popular and when the Aberdeen Ski Club ran several ski tows and even installed calor gas flood lighting for evening skiing.

That chap made my day and it was great to reminisce with him about those golden years. So, there I was, free skiing at Glenshee! A lifelong ambition fulfilled, for I had been saying for years, that the only reason I was staying alive for so long was to qualify for that particular concession.

I mentioned that little story to a great lady, Hilda Jamieson, the matriarch of the Dundee Jamieson family which was behind the opening up of the Glenshee Centre in 1962 and who still skied in her nineties. She smiled gently and whispered, *"There weren't many free tickets given out in our day"*.

Looking Back

I have touched on the story of the Glasgow and West of Scotland climbing clubs and how the likes of the Creag Dhu Mountaineering Club from Clydeside, morphed into the Glencoe Ski Club and became so important in the early developments not only in Glencoe. But, we have to go further back in time to put all this into perspective. The Scottish Ski Club was founded in 1907 by a small group of gentlemen most of whom had emerged from the Scottish Mountaineering Club, formed in 1889. In that year, at the inaugural meeting it was proposed that the club be called the Scottish Alpine Club, because it was thought that the only serious climbing of the time was in the Alps and the English, mainly the English upper class, had made many of the first ascents and popularised alpine mountain tourism.

At the public meeting in Glasgow, the proposal to call the new club the "Scottish Alpine Club", was disputed and common sense prevailed. The rest is history as the Scottish Mountaineering Club continues to flourish as does its fledgling, the Scottish Ski Club. The following letter will give you a taste of those very early days. It is from Vol. 11 of the S.M.C. Journal of 1892 and is by W.W. Naismith, a founder of the club. This is extracted from a "Century of Scottish Mountaineering". Edited by W.B. Brooker, and printed in 1988. Bill Brooker was a mountain and skiing acquaintance of mine.

On the Boards 1892

On the Campsie Fells with Norwegian Skis   By W.W. Naismith

For the sake of any uninitiated, it may be explained that skis [pron. "shes"] are wooden snow skates, 7 feet long and 3 to 4 inches wide, largely used in northern lands ... [see Dr Nanson's "Across Greenland"] ... Skis might often be employed with advantage in winter ascents in Scotland, or rather in descents ... for although Norsemen skate up, as well as down hills, few men in this country are likely to acquire such facility as to use them when going uphill, but they can easily be towed up, as they weigh only a few pounds. In the Alps it is not unlikely that the sport may eventually become popular.

Old Naismith was not wrong 120 years ago. There was another man from early in the 20th century who was also a giant in his time.

Butchart's Corrie

Col. H. D. Butchart was an Aberdonian, a member of the Scottish Mountaineering Club, a founding member of the Scottish Ski club in 1907 and later the President and, he knew his mountains. When asked by me to give some early recollections about his early days for my club annual journal, he sent me this letter in August 1960 as a contribution. You have to have various ordinance maps to hand, to follow his many detailed references to the areas he and the early Scottish Ski Club members found to ski.

Early Skiing in Scotland

Dear Rattray,

Many apologies for the delay in sending you the information asked for in your letter of 18th. March and which I promised in my letter of 28th. March to give you as far as I could.

I have not forgotten about it. But strange to say, I have been extraordinarily occupied these last few months. It is not satisfactory to do this sort of letter in bits and I could not find a suitable period until now.

Scottish skiing was practically non-existent until 1907 when a meeting was held in Edinburgh on 22nd November 1907 and was attended by representatives from Glasgow, Edinburgh, Dundee and Aberdeen. Dr. W.S. Bruce of the Scottish Antarctic Expedition was called to the chair. Mr. R.H. Winger, Dundee, read a statement giving a short history of the movement. The meeting then decided to form the Scottish Ski Club, drew up a constitution and elected officer bearers. So *far as Aberdeen was concerned, skiing had started about 1904/ 06 with Mr. W.L. Cook of John Cook and Son, who had done some ski-ing in Norway. He got Ian Mclaren of Steed and Co. to start skiing and he became the local representative of the club in Aberdeen. The original members of the club in Aberdeen in 1907 were, Henry Alexander [afterwards Lord Provost], R. Rudman Brown, H.J.Butchart, W.R. Cook, H.G. Drummond, A. and C. Fyffe, Henry Kellas, J.G. Kyd, (later Registrar General for Scotland) Ian McLaren, Ross Stewart, the total membership in Scotland in 1907 was 70.*

The next point you asked about was transport. In those days the motor car was practically non-existent we therefore had to depend on the railway and on horse vehicles. In my first expedition, we took train to Dinnet where by arrangement we were met by a waggonette and two horses. Cook, being an expert, went on his skis being towed by the waggonette. We went to Morven from a point close to Logiecoldstone and returned to Ballater on ski, down the Tullich Burn, where we got the train. Transport in the early days being so difficult, we mostly went to Ballater and skied either on the hills behind Brackly or on Morven. On one occasion, I drove by dogcart, myself driving from Dunkeld to the highest point of the road from Pitlochry to Kirkmichael, put up the horse in a hut and then skied on Ben Vrackie.

The best place for the club as a whole was Dalwhinnie. I had some very good days there on either side of the railway. On one occasion we had Vivian Caulfield who wrote probably the first book on ski-ing, "How to Ski" much of it holds good today.

Talking about skiing personalities. The first President of the club lectured to us in Aberdeen in November 1908 and E.C. Richardson came up to Scotland to encourage us. But to return to places, as the motor car came into use we in skiing, realised that the best sport was in the spring and the fact that the roads were frequently not cleared meant that we tended to go only to places where the road was clear.

On Strathdon we skied on the Meikle Geal Charn S. W. of Cockbridge, on the Moss Hill from Strathdon, on the Buck of the Cabrach. On Deeside, frequently on an afternoon as well as by moonlight on the Hill of Fare from Echt. The Corrennie Hill, really Strathdon, from the Skene, Alford road near

Tillyfourie Station and also from the Echt, Tarland road to Benaquhallie from the highest point of that road. Morven from many sides by the kindness of Keiller Greig on the fields just north of the west end of the Pass of Ballater. Blelack Hill and Craiglich from the Echt, Tarland road. The Geallaig Hill not only from Abergeldie now frequently used, but from the Gairn with the run down to the Gairn. Ben Avon by the road through Invercauld leaving the cars by the Bealach Dearg. The hills around the Sluggan when there was a bridge for moving timber behind the churchyard near Braemar Castle. Crane Drochaide by a footbridge one and a half miles west of Braemar now washed away.

Ben Macdhui from the Luibeg Burn. On the south side of the River Mongour from the Slug road, Peter Hill from the Forest of Birse road, Carnferg from the Fungle. The hills south of Ballater, Craig Vallach and Am Mullach and several times by these to Mount Keen, Lochnagar by permission of the factor, by the Glas Alt Sheil, also by Allnaguibach and by the Dansig Bridge from the Braemar road. A very good run down the Alt Corrie Dubh Burn and then down the path. Morrone used to be a favorite run from Braemar, also south of it to Carn na Droichaite. The corrie behind the shepherds house at Glen Cluny Lodge used to be very popular also Carn Dubh opposite. Then we came to use Carn Aosda and the Cairnwell and the corrie between them. (now called Butchart's Corrie) . Meall Odhar, Glas Moal. In the early days we did not go down the same run very often but rather made a tour, eg. Glas Cairn of Claise, Carn Tuirc and then the long run to Loch Callater.

It is interesting to note that in the very early days the owners or factors of Mar Forest were muchly against skiing on their property but that was overcome fairly early.

So far as dress was concerned, the most marked changes are in women's dress. Up to at least 1912 and probably up to the commencement of the first war, women wore skirts and hats of some size! I have looked up some back numbers of the club magazine and confirmed this by photographs of 1912. Men have not changed much. They wore knickerbockers or breeches with putties. A fashion came in of wearing white spats but I don't think they were ever worn in Scotland.

For the club as a whole, the Easter meets have always been the highlight. Originally they rented the old Glenmore Lodge and the gardener's wife did the cooking. Numbers increased and some had to go into the hotel in Aviemore. More numbers, and everyone went to the hotel in Aviemore. The hotel was always full to capacity until it was burned down about 1960. We skied mainly on Cairngorm with occasional tours to Ben Macdhui. We also skied on Sgor Dhu – one of the best ever Easters, and in Glen Feshie, holding our races on Carn Ban down the Alt Fearnagan.

The 1914-19 war closed down the club's activities and also killed many of our members including two of Aberdeen's origional members, Ian McLarem and Auslyn Fife. The club was not resuscitated until 1929 when 90 joined as a result of a circular, of whom, 25 were members before the war. When it closed down there were 200 members and now (in 1960) there are 1880.

I am sorry that the Aberdeen Ski Club runs on its own. The Scottish club was formed to encourage skiing throughout Scotland. It kept the flag flying between the wars when one could seldom get more than 5 or 6 people to go out. What has made skiing was the fact that men in the forces were taught to ski in Germany after the second war and when they came home they naturally wanted to continue. I trust you will get something out of this and that you will get lots of material from others for your magazine.

I shall be glad to try to answer any questions.
Yours sincerely
H. J. Butchart

Fashion Note

Ties, knickerbockers, spats and big hats were de rigeur early in the 1900s according to Harry Butchart but the first winner of the Aberdeen.S.C. Hunter-Leigh Cross Country Race Trophy held at Abergeldie in 1959 also wore a tie and a pair of the oldest plus fours or knickerbockers, still extant in Scotland at that time. These ancient breeks and their owner John Mcleod then moved to Vermont in the USA in the 1960s and have actually been spotted more recently, still skiing in the Wilmington area where they are permanently based.

Geschmozzel start on Gaelic Hill 1959

That particular race event at Abergeldie had a geschmozzel start and it was the first and only massed start ski race I ever experienced. This involved the likelihood of collisions and pile ups in the early rush to be leader and, that proved to be true. Started at 2000 feet up the Gaellic Hill at Abergeldie, there was a howling gale and because someone had inconveniently lost the stop watch and timed starts were therefore impossible, the clamour was for a quick and mass start. "Don't lets' hang about", was the cry which blew away in the gale. It was hardly a "cross country" race for it had a descent of 1000ft. over rough terrain. It was best described as a "mad dash", fearful but fun.

The first snow falls of the winter were always eagerly watched for and one autumn, Mcleod, he of the famous plus fours, now residing in Vermont," led me astray. In October 1956 the first snow falls were reported on Ben Avon and we rose early to hitch a lift in a pre-war Rolls Royce car converted to become a fast paper delivery van. It was the Sunday morning newspaper delivery van, serving the Deeside valley and, for an illegal threee bob, it dropped us off at the gates to Invercauld Castle. The slog up Glen Sluggan led us to the Glen Quoich and uphill between Beinn a' Bhuird and Ben Avon, to turn right up by the Knap or Clach a' Chleirich, the Priests or Pulpit Stone. It took three hours

The winners: John McLeod [centre] winner. Steve Stevenson [left] second. The author [right] third.

climbing but we reached the 300 metre long strip of new snow, the first of the winter. We had two runs that day before time to descend to catch the last "climber's bus" home. The things we did because of our fascination with snow! It was a form of madness perhaps.

Respect

Col. Butchart was very well known in Aberdeen, in University circles where he was Secretary to the Senate for 30 years, in Scouting as the County Commissioner and in climbing and skiing circles. I first came across him when I was 19 and serving as an Assistant Warden at the Scout Movement's permanent camping ground at Templars Park near Aberdeen. He had occasion to speak to me in his official capacity and addressed me as "Rattray".

At the time I thought this highhanded and autocratic for I had never been addressed as such before. It was only later I understood that it was just the habit of his generation, particularly with his military background. Having been brought up in a scout group which rather eschewed officialdom and while playing the scouting game vigorously we avoided getting too close to those who ruled from above.

Then, a few years later when I heard him make a case for joining the Scottish Ski Club Aberdeen branch instead of forming our independent Aberdeen Ski Club early in 1956, I saw another side to him. He was genuinely disappointed when we chose to go it alone and wished us well. Later again when he penned that detailed account of the early days of skiing for our club journal, I understood more about the man. Even later when I read of his mountaineering days I could not but put him on a pedestal.

He was the first to establish a marker for the ascent of the six highest mountains in the Cairngorms in 1908. Starting from Loch Builg, he and his four companions, climbed Ben Avon, Ben a' Bhuird, Cairngorm, Ben Macdhui, Cairntoul and Braeriach in 19 hours and they had covered 28 miles and 9000 vertical feet. Their record has been whittled away over the century, but they did it first! Fifty years later I came across him on a cloud shrouded Glas Maol. My little group had stopped to catch our breath and to consult a map, when we heard the rattle of steel edges on ice. From out the mist a bulky figure skied past us and down into the murk. It was Harry Butchart, who must have been in his 70s and was in full control, alone and in atrocious conditions. Yes, I did look up to that gentleman, Scout leader, mountaineer and skier.

Falling Gracefully

My age group had used skis for some years before ski tows came on the scene, but only as an adjunct to climbing. We climbed and carried skis, utilising ex-army skis with WD issue "skins" and old Kandahar bindings. The hope was that after the climb we could have some downhill running on the way home. That would have been straight running, because none in our wee group could turn ... without falling, especially in deep snow.

The art was to traverse across the hill, stop and then perform a kick turn and continue on the opposite traverse. Skiers today spend most of their time on prepared pistes and are seldom faced with crusty old snow, drifted into banks in places, with clumps of heather and the occasional rocks to add interest. Falling became a very fine art and some could actually achieve it gracefully. In the Scottish Mountaineering Club Anthology edited by Bill Brooker, I also found a perfect description of the struggles to master the wooden boards ... just to have a few minutes of glorious downhill running.

"We would get to the top of the hill, put on our skis and swung, slipped, staggered, fell, leaped, bounced, collided, crashed, ploughed, rose, groped, slithered, fell again, smacked, knelt, tottered, sprawled, lost a ski, overtook it, put it on, spun, collapsed, waded, dived, gasped, blew, dropped, rolled, bounded and finally arrived breathless at the bottom".

For everyone in the 1950s, the climb from Glenmore to the foot of the Corrie Cas took nearly two hours of stiff walking/climbing, carrying skis and rucsac. It was possible if you were fit, to enjoy perhaps seven or eight runs down the full length of the Cas in a day, before the trek back down to Glenmore. The uphill climb back to the top of the Cas slope, could take 30 minutes and the downhill run, five or so minutes. No roads, no ski tows!

Yellow Snow

Skiing can be thirsty work and so it was always tempting to scoop up a little snow to quench a dry mouth. But experience taught us to be more discerning. Lesson one was, "never eat yellow snow", and that had always been a little joke among snow users. But when black snow or even orange snow began to appear on the higher slopes, there were questions which needed to be answered. In 1987 accusations of government inaction and neglect were raised when the MP for Inverness, Nairn and Lochaber, Russell Johnston, threatened to cause an election issue about pollution over the Cairngorms. He accused the then Scottish Office Environment Minister, Michael Ancram of giving priority to short-term financial considerations over the long-term good of the environment. The problem was Black Snow on the Cairngorms ... the first scientifically recorded evidence of the phenomenon anywhere in the world.

An East Anglia University team was investigating the area for evidence of acid rain and its variations, black snow, believed to be caused by industrial pollution swept over from factories in Southern Britain and industrial Europe. Their evidence showed that it contained elements of fossil fuel capable of wiping out fish stocks in hill lochs and even of killing entire forests. I subsequently saw evidence of trees dying off in the Aosta Valley region in the Italian Alps which was only a couple of hours rail time from major industrial centres by Turin.

The Small Clubs

The fascination with mountains has always been deep in the heart of the Scottish psyche, witness the many, many books in every bookshop. Snow adds another dimension and when skiing became possible for "ordinary folk," the response was truly amazing. I have described what happened between 1950 and 1990 as "The Glory Days of Scottish Skiing". It did become a true movement, which pulled in people from all social groupings, all ages and inclinations. Clubs large and small sprung into being, some to become large, permanent fixtures and some to last for a few years, until they were amalgamated or disbanded. In Aberdeenshire alone, small clubs flourished including in Elgin, Peterhead, Fraserburgh, Stonehaven, Banchory, Ballater, Braemar, Inverurie, Moray, Keith, Turriff, Braemar and Huntly, etc.

Keith Ski Club fell into that latter category and their particular story was typical of many others across Scotland. The story begins during the Second World War when Canadian soldiers were billeted and worked as foresters, near Keith an Aberdeenshire market town, some 35 miles from today's Lecht Ski Centre and 45 miles from Aberdeen.

The local boys were fascinated by these Canadians, some of whom had skis and shared the nearby low ground slopes of the town with the boys and their sledges. Sandy Gauld was one of the lads who got the chance to stand on the back of a soldier's skis and he told his story in 1997 in the Scots Magazine. He and a friend, Bill Milne were the first of the local young men who bought ex-army skis and sticks after the war and they progressed to cross-country skiing on nearby hills.

Then the bigger mountains beckoned, more joined their group and a club was formed called the Keith Outdoor Club. Soon they had built a tow of 200 metres length using the ubiquitous Fergie tractor to tow up to12 skiers at a time. It was used on local farm fields and then the machine was moved to Lecht, to the very site occupied today by the Ski Centre which operates on the highest point of the hill pass at 2050 ft. The tractor venture started off badly, for to get the machine onto the slope, it had to cross some soft ground by the road side just as the Aberdeen Club Ferguson tractor did a short time later. The Keith machine sank into the bog. It too was pulled out and went on to be well used. At the end of that 1959/60 season, the tractor had a "mishap" and crashed on the way home to Keith never to operated again. The lads moved on, joining the Moray Ski Club to use that club's tows, and so the Keith Club ceased to exist. That story was repeated time and again across Scotland. However, until I began to research this book I did not realise just how many ski clubs still exist in this new century and how different their functions are today.

Blanket clouds

The chairlift companies never had an easy ride. They were at the mercy of a fickle climate as anyone who has been on a Scottish mountain can vouch for. When the weather is good, skiers and climbers can have the most delightful experiences in both winter and summer. When the winds blow, and the rain and sleet drive into our faces, drenching and chilling us to the bone, our views change. But what would life be without challenge? I have always said that on the good days, when the snow lies deep and even, the skiing was as good as we could have anywhere. Conversely, when weather is bad, it can be sheer hell ... bloody awful in fact. To be at 3000 feet or higher on any Scottish mountain when the winds blow and the wind chill factor is high, the spindrift blows so hard that you can barely see, and, the snow is glazed to ice rink consistency so that few skiers, if any, can get a steel edge to hold. That is the time to go home. Tomorrow is another day.

"Tomorrow arrives and all the towns and cities are in deep mourning as the mist and clouds blanket the land ... not worth even thinking about going to the hill!. Or so it seems to the faint hearts and those who choose to lie abed. It's a long drive to the hills and the road is familiar but, still the mists hang over the hills and obliterate any distant views. On the Glenmore to Cairngorm ski road, there are cars with skis coming back down and heading home and, doubts increase. Are we on a wasted journey? In the car park, visibility is down to 100 metres and vague shapes loom around the cars. But, in for a penny, in for a pound! Up we go on the chairlift, the annual lift pass has been paid for ... sorry to waste it.

Just three pylons up the White Lady, the sky seems slightly lighter, the mist slightly less damp. Just at the fifth pylon, something magical happens. A golden orb appears overhead out of the mist and suddenly we come out of the misty blanket and suddenly, the entire world is white. Every top, every gully is white with fresh snow. It's a skier's dreamland and to think we nearly stayed in bed! If you are a mountain person, then I am preaching to the converted, for you will have experienced that happy phenomenon when the valleys and the glens, are cloaked in a dense cotton wool blanket which obscures everything. Only the brave and the energetic will struggle to climb through the fog to see what lies above.

It was W.H. Murray, the Scottish mountaineer and famed writer who said,

"Mountains throw into high relief, a beauty that fairly takes the eyes by storm ... but effort must be expended, sacrifices must be faced; without these, only imaginary mountains are climbed."

In midsummer the same cloud phenomena can happen and for the many who still climb to see the rising sun on the longest day of the year, it can be so dramatic. From Aberdeen we usually favoured Lochnagar which was easy of access and, from the Angus Glens, folk from Dundee and Forfar would walk over the old Jock's Road hill path to Loch Muick to join others on the trek to the top at 1155metres. My earliest memory was of a miserable climb through wet mist in the night when we seriously thought of aborting and going back to the tent. Then we had the cold wait among the boulders on the summit crag until the false dawn slowly brightened the northern sky at around 3.45 am.. Then the sun emerged over the Morayshire coast to reveal a complete white blanket of puffy cloud stretching in all directions to the horizon. The valleys were entirely hidden and only the major peaks of the central Cairngorms pushed up through the blanket of cloud. An astonishing sight and it was as though one could step out over and onto the mattress of cloud. And, to think we nearly stayed in bed!

Skiing? That's uncool !

We began this look back at the last sixty years on our mountains and inevitably we realise that life was very different indeed in the early days. In the first two decades after the war, money was tight, pleasures were simpler, few of us owned cars and cheap flights from Scottish airports to warm or cold climes, just were not available. Oh, and television in it's infancy, did not glue bottoms to settees. We did not see too many "couch potatoes" in the early days. Which brings to mind a painful lesson one old man had to learn. Taking a grandson up his first ever "Munro" at the age of thirteen and also to Chamonix to experience skiing in the Alps, Grandpa naturally wanted to hear how the boy's friends at school had reacted to his adventures. *"Oh, I never told them,"* he said, *"They wouldn't have thought me cool."* Wow! what is it with the new generation? I would have given an arm and a leg at his age to have had such adventures. But, then was then and now is now.

Aberdeen Ski Club at the Cairngorm Ski Night TV programme

Billy Connelly

Following its sponsorship of racing in Scotland over several seasons Grampian Television also capitalised on the general buzz surrounding the sport and produced a light entertainment programme called "Cairngorm Ski Nights" which became very popular and which ran for several series over three years. The format was based on the "apres ski" theme and many well known musicians and entertainers were booked to appear.

Billy Connelly was just at the start of his career and he appeared in one show as the guitar player and singer in the Humble Bums, a duo, then just coming onto the music circuits, long before he went solo as a comedian. Several Scottish traditional artists made appearances with Highland dancing and singing, shades of the White Heather Club, that old and very popular show in its day. Popular music brought the likes of Kiki Dee on to the Grampian TV screen and several other new talents went on to become big names. Jimmy Spankie the newscaster at Grampian TV was the anchor man acting as the genial host throughout the series

The programmes were recorded and skiers from clubs all over Scotland made up the audiences. All the big clubs were invited and arrangements were made to bus them, two coach loads at a time to the television studios in Aberdeen. The stage set was simple with the invited audience dressed in sweaters and ski pants and the occasional bobble hat. There was music and some dancing but the professional artists were the main attraction. It was a successful format and many clubs from around the country had their 30 minutes of television fame.

The coaches came from Inverness and from Dumfries, from Glasgow and Edinburgh, from the Borders and even from Newcastle and Carlisle. The series was so popular that it was sold by Grampian TV to the north England regional television companies and the ski clubs in those areas were invited. It was a long haul for them but few clubs refused the invitations, despite the many hours travel involved. Grampian paid for the coach travel and the administration costs and the skiers were given modest hospitality during the recorded entertainment. It was artificial and staged of course but, it was popular entertainment and captured the mood of the time.

Chapter 17

Mar Lodge

Flights of Fancy

Mar Lodge was very much in the news from 1963 and sadly, it was a story of serious endeavour but glorious failure. The Lodge lies five miles west of Braemar and just south of Beinn a' Bhuird, a bulky 1196 metre mountain adjoining Ben Avon, lying north west of Braemar. The Lodge, was built by Queen Victoria for one of her daughters, Princess Louise in the 1890's. In 1959, the entire estate was divided after the death of the last royal, Princess Alice. The main Mar Lodge Estate was then bought by the Anglo-Swiss bankers, the Panchaud brothers, Gerald and John. Initially they planned to use the vast estate with its elegant Lodge, encompassing vast areas of the Central Cairngorms, for private hunting, shooting and fishing.

From 1959 until 1963, there was a series of snowy winters with much low ground snow and long ski seasons. This contributed to the euphoria and the confidence which was gripping the skiing movement in Scotland. The Panchaud brothers were caught up in the excitement and they were persuaded to explore the possibilities of a ski development, by the then Chairman of Aberdeen Ski Club, Richard E. Jackson who was Chief Executive of a large vehicle and garage company in Aberdeen.

Dick had a brother who was an architect and between them, they had a dream. They also had the ears and financial backing of the Swiss bankers at Mar Lodge and the infectious enthusiasm of a thrusting and growing ski club. If Mar Lodge had in fact become a successful ski centre, there would still have been plenty of space for the hunting and

Mar Lodge with the ski centre behind the lodge

shooting brigade … approximately 100 square miles of it.

The plans were researched, enthusiasm was stoked and the dream for the first low-ground ski centre in Scotland was launched. Two Swiss built tows were imported and erected, tree stumps and rocks were removed from slopes ready for the snow makers to blast out artificial snow when real snow was in short supply. In fact, snow guns produce "real" snow, only artificial, in that it is produced by blasting out compressed air and water together, through nozzles, when the air temperature is at 0 degrees centigrade or less. The compressors for the snow blowers were housed in a new Swiss style chalet building among trees just behind the elegant Mar Lodge ballroom. Ironically, just as the entire project was failing, a couple of years later, the machine house was awarded a national architectural prize for its sensitive blending with its environment.

This preview news item about Mar Lodge was released by management, to the national and regional press in 1963.

Mar Lodge

The Lodge itself, around which everything is planned, is well sheltered by huge pines and the specially tailored ski slopes lie immediately above these woods. Here, the red deer roam in large numbers and eagles are not uncommon. A hundred yards from the Lodge, among trees, there are two ski lifts. Both are T-bar tows, the Blue tow has a capacity of 600 per hour and the Red tow has a capacity of 800 per hour with a vertical height of 600 feet. The snow making machinery will be used to cover an area of 20 acres, producing powdery or granular snow at the rate of 5,600 cu. ft. per hour as conditions require. The climate of the district enables the machinery to operate effectively for the entire length of the ski season in Scotland, with the capacity to extend it several weeks.

Instruction will be by professional instructors from the Ski School d'Ecosse [Frith Finlayson's Aviemore School which has opened a branch with Alan Flett as director] A huge car park in front of the Lodge will hold over 1000 vehicles and a bus company has agreed to extend services if required. The back of the Lodge has been completely reconstructed with two restaurants, ski shop and hire, changing rooms and showers and first-aid room. In addition, the historic ballroom decorated with 365 stags heads around the wood lined hall will be open for dancing and evening entertainment, with a fully licensed bar. The chapel adjoining the Lodge will be open for skier's services. A children's creche will be fully equipped in two rooms in the Lodge and it is planned to build a floodlit curling and skating rink.

Scottish skiing has been neglected in the past. It is not the lack of suitable slopes nor conditions nor enthusiasm, but the lack of all the necessary amenities in one compact area. This year, Mar Lodge is offering the beginnings of a ski resort. With the help of ski clubs and the growing public interest it can quickly develop into a resort that will compare with any on the Continent.

Confident words indeed and, there was a degree of super optimism and fantasy in the air. It is not on record what Mr Robert Clyde, the General Manager of the Cairngorm Development had to say about these grand plans for Mar Lodge. With his own hard experiences and pioneering work on the other side of the Cairngorms, I would hazard a guess that in his own blunt way, he would have been less than enthusiastic, sceptical perhaps. Many others took a very large pinch of salt and muttered, "we will wait and see how Mar Lodge works out." At Glenshee, David Jamieson and his Manager, David Patterson said little about the plans for the Mar Lodge Centre. If successful, it would have given skiers more choices, but would have been competition for the Glenshee set up. As for me, I was prepared to dream for a good outcome as were others in the Aberdeen Club who volunteered to train for the first aid team and rescue unit at Mar Lodge.

The whole project was based on the premise that Braemar was one of the coldest villages in Britain; with around 138 days of frost at village level, and 100 days with lying snow each year. But, local experience, only voiced after the failure of the project two years on, showed that certain little areas could buck the trend and "warm hollows" could exist as did "frost hollows". This is where thermal inversions can take place, and Mar Lodge, lying by the fast flowing River Dee, was in just such a "warm hollow", with a tendency to be frost free. Typical of local comment was one worthy from Inverey, the small village close to the Lodge who said, *"If they'd jist askit me, I could have "telt" them a' aboot that."*

The project went ahead and opened with a flourish just before Christmas 1963. There was a little natural snow for a week or two but everyone was full of hope and expectations. The other facilities around Mar Lodge were much admired, but still the snow did not arrive from the skies or from the snow guns. The snow making installation was hailed as the largest in Europe, [at that time] but the technology was still at the development stage. Today, snow making, with greatly improved technology, is common-place at most of the alpine resorts, and in using guns, or at least snow cannons or blowers, which distribute the new snow more evenly, to augment bare and worn sections of the runs. Shortage of snow is not unique to Scotland. Many European and North American centres suffer from shortages at critical times which can be financially embarrassing.

Oh for a Piste Beastie

Critical to all snow making success in any ski centre today, is firstly frost and then the use of modern piste machines which groom the snow as it is produced and spread it evenly across the slopes. Those of us who are privileged to ski in alpine resorts will know the magical sight, of twinkling head lamps late at night, working on the high ski slopes, as the piste machines groom the slopes in preparation for the next day. A far cry from the reality of Scottish skiing in its early days.

These sophistications were not available in 1964 as Jimmy Reid, the assistant estate manager and engineer in charge, found to his dismay. He told me about one of his early attempts to produce snow when he ran the snow guns at full blast one night at the cost in power of £300-£3000, at today's costs. With no machine to level and spread the large mound of snow, it thawed slowly in the warmth of the sun next day and then the next night it froze solidly to become an un-skiable; mound of hard snow, covered in ice. There were then problems with the water supply from the River Dee and other teething problems as with any new project.

Little natural snow fell on low ground that winter of 1963/4 with little frost or snow on the slopes behind the Lodge, while higher slopes on the Central Cairngorms also saw scarcity of snow. In contrast, the previous four years had seen excellent ski conditions across Scotland and many weeks of great low ground snow cover and continuous frosts. During that four year period, the plans for Mar Lodge had been hatched and building completed. Sadly, the project opened just at the end of 1963 and the next year, 1964 was the poorest snow and frost year for a decade. Nature can be so fickle.

Earlier attempts to attract skiers to upper Deeside also failed in 1931. Following several good ski seasons the two principal hotels in Braemar the Invercauld Arms and the Fife Arms combined to bring in a couple of horse drawn sleighs and groups of musician while advertising ski holidays in the national press. The expected snow falls did not come and the project failed.

Arraba

My own experiences on manufactured snow proved to be magnificent. It was 1989 and we opted to ski the Sella Ronda region of the Dolomites, basing ourselves in Arraba. It was early January and the snow was scarce but we had contracted, so off we had to go. From Venice airport we drove up into the high valleys to arrive to no snow. After the initial dismay we were told that we would be bussed each day to the village of St. Vigilio and to ski the Kronplatz … the where? That small mountain proved to be an oasis in a vast snowless desert. Several kilometres of superb pistes immaculately groomed to allow fast cruising. There were black, red and blue runs to please everyone and no ice and no queues. And the sun shone! Dozens of snow cannons blasted out the white stuff every night to prove the point that the man-made snow is first class, if the technology is.

Snow makers at Kronplatz near Arabba in north Italy

Ben a Bhuird

Mar Lodge opened in December 1963 and virtually shut down 24 months later. But, I did ski there, briefly, on real snow and then even more briefly on hard frozen, man-made snow. We also skied on Beinn a' Bhuird the huge mountain just six miles north, on a few occasions as the club was undertaking the early snow surveys and when one or two races were held.. On one occasion Dundee and Aberdeen were organising a joint race and we had invited the Aberdeen Mountain Rescue Team to join us and provide back-up in event of skiing accidents. It was a good day and four of the rescue team were amusing themselves by glissading down on a large plastic bag when something went very wrong. Their brake man had his ice axe to control the descent but they hit a bump, bounced, lost control and in the ensuing tumble, he stabbed himself in the chest and punctured a lung.

It was ironic that the team had to carry one of their own off the hill that day. In my young climbing days I had been recruited into the Aberdeen Mountain Rescue Team. It was in the 1950s, long before such teams became established, organised or equipped. We were very loosely associated with the two Aberdeen climbing clubs, the Cairngorm and the Etchecan Clubs and when there was a police call out in the middle of the night to search for a lost climber, one fellow climber was the police contact man and he would ring round and try to get a few others to volunteer to join the local police and gamekeepers. If it was a Sunday night and we had just come back from the hills, some would refuse to go out again. The thought of carrying a heavy stretcher over rough terrain was also a deterrent and those who could lose a day's wage were also put off, except if the missing person was known to them. There was no organisation, no transport, no radios, no recognition, just a handful of volunteers willing to go out just for the hell of it.

Fatalities

Mcleod and I were there when one of the biggest mountain tragedies happened in 1959. Five from the Glasgow Outdoor Club had set off from Braemar on New Year's Day to walk over the hills to Glen Doll, a trip of some 12 miles but over a high plateau at between 2,500 and 3000 ft. Ignoring the forecast for high winds and snow they set off late in the day and literally disappeared for three months, until the snow melted to reveal their bodies. The oldest walker was the first to collapse; the rest carried on but dropped one by one and were buried in the snow. The youngest, just seventeen, got to within 400 yards of a hill pony shelter above Glen Doll before he too dropped and died.

We could see the frozen footsteps of the party as they had climbed up from Loch Callater to gain the plateau, where the blizzard covered all tracks and eventually overcame them. They had broken all the obvious rules for survival. They could have turned back or dug in and sheltered for the night. But they were badly equipped and inexperienced. Oddly enough one newspaper report suggested that they were experienced climbers and well equipped. We on the spot thought differently and put that report down to bad reporting. But then, none of us were "well equipped" in those days, in comparison to today's clothing and equipment There were other call outs, some with happy endings but some also with more tragedy. But that is another story.

Avalanche on Sgor Mor

Avalanches can be scary and fatal. My own baptism by snow came early in my climbing life. It was on Sgor Mor half way up Glen Clunie from Braemar. It was winter 1947/8 and my first ever winter climb and the Etchecan Climbing Club bus could only get to Clunie Lodge just 6 miles from Braemar where snow blocked the road. The old shooting lodge had been used by the military during the war but was due for demolition.

The snow was deep but the sun shone and so it was a good day to be on any hill. We floundered for a mile or more up by Baddoch Burn and then started up towards the summit at 887 metres. It was a shallow gully which looked innocuous enough but when our group of 15 was strung out across the top third of the hill there was a crack and a rumble. My best mate and I were last in the line because we were rookies, and we had just stepped off a rocky outcrop onto the snow filled gully when the slide struck. We just had time to stick axes into the snow and rock and we were merely swept off our feet and showered by snow and debris.

The snow carried five of our group down 400 feet and for a moment after, there was complete silence. Then we careered down to help. There were legs and heads visible and we scraped and dug them all out to reveal the injures. The most serious was a fractured skull, the others, broken and dislocated bones, serious lacerations and bruises. Two went off to seek help but our bus had gone back to Braemar and that took some time. We carried and helped the wounded down to the Baddoch and an empty and damp old shepherd's cottage where we broke in and lit a fire. The seriously injured man was unconscious in between spells of delirium and agitation when he had to be restrained and we wedged a spoon in his mouth to stop him swallowing his tongue. It was obvious that many of the injuries were caused by ice axes attached to wrists thrashing about in the avalanche.

I spent half hourly shifts tending to the man as he thrashed about. The secretary of the climbing club had a dislocation and required 50 stitches in her scalp when hospitalised, while on the spot we could only treat the injured as best we could. The ambulance arrived 5 hours later and then we carried some casualties through the deep snow a mile to the road. It was a baptism for me for it was my first time applying first-aid … for real. Andy and I had all the Scout badges, now it was a very real experience! We looked after our own Assistant Scout Leader who had first taken us to climb the sea cliffs near Aberdeen and we make his arm injury and scalp wounds comfortable. I was 17, barely 18 years old but I grew up very quickly that day.

Abergeldie

Four good snow years I have already talked about, between 1959-63, saw the Aberdeen Club adopt the roadside fields at Abergeldie, near Balmoral Castle

Abergeldie rope tow prices 1959

on Deeside, running a few small ski tows and then tractors. In the winter 1962/3 there were 10 weeks of near perfect conditions through February and March and into April. The road south beyond Braemar was seldom fully opened and our club was geared up for the hoped-for conditions at Abergeldie. Fencing had been taken down in expectation and tracks opened for skiers to climb Gaellaig Hill {743metres} and descend to the lower slopes and the ski tows, without interruption. A small tow was also being operated on the big hill above the fields.

The tenant farmer was obliging and cooperative but, by the end of that winter, the County Council was raising problems. Firstly there were fears about road congestion at Abergeldie. As many as 800 skiers could arrive at weekends and with limited nearby off-road parking, many cars were parking on the A93 road itself. Frequent snow during the period, covered the main road which lies at around 900ft. above sea level, for long periods This caused problems for the police. Then there were concerns about public sanitation.

The club had also investigated the need for this and plans were in hand for temporary loos, for the following season.

A more powerful Fordson tractor tow served the adjoining fields for those 10 weeks and was a huge attraction. So good were the skiing conditions at Abergeldie with deep snow and sunshine, topped up by frequent night time frosts and snow falls, that calor gas lighting was hired and installed to allow evening skiing to take place on certain nights of the week.

Negotiations went on with the County Council, who even considered building permanent public toilets and car parking nearby. The weather pattern, the following season 1964, reverted to the more normal when Mar Lodge failed and to my knowledge, the Abergeldie fields were never used by the club again. Occasional touring skiers are still seen on the hill and the good memories of the past, still linger. There is a small stone cairn at the foot of the fields today and just 40 metres from the road. Who built it I know not. But I like to think it was erected for someone who had good memories of those great days at Abergeldie.

Snow clearing

In the early 1960s the road from Braemar to the Devil's Elbow, was still not being adequately snow cleared, principally because Aberdeenshire County Council lacked enough modern snow ploughs and they also had a first priority to clear roads between populated areas, however small. This was one of the first problems addressed by the new Scottish National Ski Council, a Federation of ski clubs. The Glenshee Chairlift Company lifts and facilities were ready to operate but the public on many occasions could not reach the facilities because of territorial disputes existing between County Councils. The SNSC was able to inject some urgency into the matter. Logic would dictate that heavy snow falls are best cleared from above, not uphill on steep roads. This meant that powerful machines needed to be stationed at the summit of the hill pass. By tradition, the available snow ploughs were stationed at Ballater, Braemar, Spittal of Glenshee and Blairgowrie to serve low ground centres of population. On the south side of the hill pass, the gradient was severe and the actual Devil's Elbow was a fearsome tight Z bend.

The fact that all the main facilities at the Glenshee Centre were actually on the Aberdeenshire side of the boundary line and therefore legally in Glen Clunie caused immense problems for the administrators and local politicians. Perth and Kinross was therefore reluctant to spend money on road improvements and snow clearing, when no council rates came into their coffers. This was despite the fact that the majority of the skiers bringing business to the Chairlift Company, came from the south and not Aberdeenshire.

For several years, Aberdeenshire went ahead and straightened long sections of the mountain road from Braemar, in its jurisdiction, while Perth and Kinross dragged their feet and consequently, many miles between Blairgowrie and the Cairnwell summit, are still tortuous in places and badly pot-holed following the winter of 2009/10. The fearsome "Elbow" had long since gone.

Road Chaos

There may well have been other legal or technical problems facing these councils. But in the eyes of thousands of frustrated skiers, from North and South, it was seen as bloody mindedness and incompetence. Meanwhile, snow ploughs failed to work together, one side seemingly refusing to cooperate with the other, when conditions called for combined efforts and shared tasks. No one would work in the other region. The result was skiers could not reach the waiting facilities and were turned away from a day's sport.

Road chaos on many occasions could only happen, and it did. Roads were ploughed only to fill in rapidly with drifting snow, when it became impossible to continue. This problem was understood only too well by the skiing fraternity, and as a Scottish Ski Council spokesman, I was quoted as saying that greater efforts should be made to keep the Devil's Elbow road open for skiers at weekends. As a result I had my fingers rapped by a council snow plough driver based in Braemar, in a letter to the Scotsman Editor. I was accused of criticising snow plough drivers, who had an already dangerous job and "all for my own selfish pleasure".

That's what happens when one sticks ones neck above the parapet. As a journalist, one gets used to slings and arrows! Over many years reporting racing in Scotland and in the Alps and also in general feature work, I found the same danger lurking. Parents in particular could be critical of under reporting of junior events or worse still, if I got a race time or even a spelling wrong.

Cairngorm had only one road authority to deal with and snow clearing problems were fewer than at Glenshee. With exceptions! In 1962 the Cairngorm ski road from Loch Morlich to the foot of Corrie Cas at the 2000ft level, was snow blocked for 42 days. That was a salutary lesson, for the budget for snow clearing machines had to be increased and dedicated for use on the high level ski road.

Chapter 18

Mountain Developments

Euphoria

Development is a dirty word in this new century but, in 1966, planners were eagerly looking at recreational opportunities, including expanding skiing facilities. The report of the Technical Group of the Scottish Development Agency contributed to the work to identify further suitable snow areas for development. Landscape, conservation and preservation were all reviewed by the Scottish Office together with population, employment and land use The final report was produced by HMSO in 1967. Twenty years later, some said the in-depth report was, "interesting, but not particularly relevant". But, in 1967 it was very relevant because many had come to realise that access to the mountains, in summer and winter was of considerable economic value and major social importance.

In the beginning government bodies were being swept along by the euphoria and the excitement of the skiing movement. Few voices from environmentalists were heard, that was to come later. The call was for more rapid development and Government was in agreement for it would bring new jobs and new prosperity to the unemployment black spots in rural and highland areas. I have described the excitement created by the rush to the snow mountains and I have emphasised the major benefits it brought to society as a whole in Scotland and especially for young people. The mountains for many were new playgrounds when leisure and recreation was in the air.

The Conservation lobby was growing slowly and in the 1960s and 70s their voice was only a whisper drowned out by the clamour for winter sports. By 1985 that movement had found a voice and had gathered momentum and influence. Attitudes changed and, while local government was pushing for more mountain development to satisfy demand, other bodies were creating resistance movements. Lurchers Gully was known to climbers and skiers for 100 years, as a fine snow holding area which also gave climbers intent on getting up onto the Cairngorm-Ben Macdhui sub-arctic plateau, comparatively easy access. Various bodies produced plans for enlargement of ski areas and more facilities on the basis of the existing demand. But Lurchers became a bitter battleground over the years.

As early as 1962 the Scottish Development Department issued circular No:2/1962 covering two matters the Secretary of State for Scotland considered of major importance, regarding outdoor recreation. Meanwhile the Scottish skiing revolution was exploding onto the scene while the politicians were discussing what to do. In 1967 the Scottish Office issued the final report of its Technical Group on the Cairngorm Area of the Eastern Highlands of Scotland under the Chairmanship of Mr. F.J. Evans, O.B.E. of the Regional Planning Office. The membership of that technical group was drawn from the Scottish Development Department, Regional Planning Officers, County Planning Officers from Aberdeen, Inverness, Banff, Moray and Nairn and Perth and Kinross. In addition, twenty nine other bodies were invited to give evidence and advice. The 1967 Report covered every aspect, from population and employment, land use, communications, roads and rail, tourist provision and recreation, landscapes, conservation and preservation and capital costs and conclusions.

The in-depth survey covered many aspects with emphasis on the tourist provision and recreation of the whole area encompassing 1,535 square miles of the Cairngorm Area of the Eastern Highlands. Bodies, including the Scottish National Ski Council took part and we, including myself, were called to the Scottish Office to give the point of view of the many clubs and individuals we represented and, the results of our own researches and findings. National and local government, the leisure and tourist industries, educational bodies and business, all saw the need for more facilities. The 1967 Report echoed the up-beat enthusiasm of the time.

That document then gather dust in the Scottish office. A fifty page, Report of a Survey of Potential Development of Beinn a' Bhuird, by Glasgow University came out in 1968 but the report was lengthy and inconclusive. In 1969 a bulky but wide ranging document entitled Royal Grampian Country, produced by the department of Geography at Aberdeen University reproduced the Glasgow report essentially in its entirety. Both were merely distillations of the Cairngorm Area Report of 1967. In 1969 a Report on Winter Sports Development on Ben Wyvis, was produced by county councillors, hotel owners, estate owner, tourist organisations and, the Forestry Commission, among others. All pipe dreams overtaken by time.

Dreams and Super Optimism

In his forward to the 1967 Report, Willie Ross, the fiery Secretary of State for Scotland welcomed the work and warmly commended it for study, for it provided invaluable background for those who would be concerned in the future developments of the Cairngorm Area. He hoped the report would, *"stimulate the imagination of the nation"*. Many organisations took part, including federations, societies, commissions, associations, trusts, boards, unions, universities and companies.

The scope of the review was very wide, even road and rail communications were studied, and specific mention was made for a Lurchers Gully spur road off the existing Cairngorm road. Lurcher's was described as having a main ski run over one and a quarter miles, suitable for average skiers. It could have a skier capacity comparable to Coire Cas, it was more suitable for novice skiers and it had better protection from prevailing winds. Even Coire Raibert was listed as having good spring skiing often lasting into June. All this indicated just how high were expectations in the 1960s and that the pressure was on, for further developments to take place as queues built up at peak times in the season.

Looking back, I find it astonishing how upbeat everyone was, including the mandarins in the Scottish Office. Grand plans for the future laid out on paper looked wonderful, take this excerpt for instance from the 1967 Cairngorm Area Report.

The Glen Feshie Road

A two lane road nearly 32 miles in length of which 21 miles would be a completely new construction and, 11 miles improved existing roads, is proposed from the trunk road A9 at Kingussie in the west to Braemar in the east via Ruthven Barracks, Drumguish, Glen Feshie, the Geldie Burn, the River Dee from the White Bridge to Linn of Dee. The existing road B970 from Ruthven Barracks to Drumguish would have to be improved; improvements on the existing road from Linn of Dee to Braemar are currently being carried out. This would be a major trans-Scotland route, linking the east and west coast ports of Aberdeen and Mallaig and would bring the Aberdeenshire and Banffshire forests within range of the pulp and paper mills at Fort William. The road would make a useful tourist route through the central massif, and if built simultaneously with the winter sports developments in the eastern part of the area, [Beinn a' Bhuird], would provide for movement between these and the Glenmore skiing centre. It has been estimated that the new improved roads from Kingussie to Braemar if constructed to provide an 18 foot carriageway, will cost not less that £2,000,000 at current prices.

The report went on to outline the need to open up the Corrie na Ciste area on Cairngorm. This project was in fact completed 1973, with a spur road of one mile leading to large parking areas and a modern café and toilet complex. Lift access followed, linking up with the earlier White Lady system and giving access to the upper Ciste bowl. Sadly all those facilities had now been closed and are becoming derelict.

Braemar and the Eastern Cairngorms

Braemar and the Ben a' Bhuird areas were then examined in the Report. Following the Mar Lodge failure with its low ground, manmade snow project, the estate owners continued to look at other alternatives for development and Ben a' Bhuird was the obvious choice For many years eyes had been cast at the huge bulk of the mountain and it's close neighbour Ben Avon, both over 1100 metres in height, with multiple tops and good snow holding gullies and corries.

While the Mar Estate was still striving to get its low ground ski centre project off the ground with the use of snow making machines, it was encouraging Aberdeen Ski Club to go ahead with a snow survey of the big mountain six miles up Glen Quoich and to the north of the Lodge. In the summer of 1964 a team of Aberdeen skiers set up a series of scaffold poles with measured markings, and for four years, teams of two, surveyed the slopes every two weeks throughout each winter. They slogged the six miles to the foot of the mountain to record depth, condition and area of snow, wind speeds and direction.

Photographs were taken from fixed points on each occasion. The complete survey was an integral part of a report by Glasgow University Geography Department, financed by the Scottish Tourist Board. Essentially the survey showed that the snowfields compared very favourably with that at other, developed ski areas. And, importantly, without the need for snow fencing. Runs varied from steep descents of short length to gentle runs of up to 4 miles with a vertical drop of 2,400 feet. Approximately 15 square miles of the mountain is above 2,000 feet and half of this area is above 3,000 feet. Alan Burnett the Secretary and then Chairman of Aberdeen S.C. took part in that lengthy survey together with Lindsay Durno, a talented young club skier who became an instructor before emigrating to British Columbia. The last we heard about him in 2009, he was Operations Manager at the Olympic Park on Mount Whistler.

Ben a' Bhuird Report

While further investigation is required it already appears from the survey and inspection that the potential of the long lasting snows of the mountain is at least equal to those of Cairngorm. Access to Bein a' Bhuird of the type already provided to Cairngorm does not exist and will need to be provided. This can be achieved in alternative ways.

{1} By the construction of a new road five miles in length through Glen Quaich to a suitable point on the western flank of Ben a' Bhuird. This road is estimated to cost £250,000. In addition, a car park would cost £10,000. Improvements of the existing 3.5 miles of public road between Linn of Dee and the foot of Glen Quaich would also be needed at an estimate of £105,000, giving a total of £325,000

{2} By the reconstruction of the existing estate road through Glen Lui, between Linn of Dee and Derry Lodge over a length of 3 miles at a cost of £175,000 and the cost of a new road over the Clais Fhearnaig into Glen Quaich, this 3 mile road would be estimated at £325,000.

The planners obviously had the bit between their teeth and astonishing plans were being considered for new road systems all over the Central Highlands. In the same report, they looked at the feasibility of a new road between Nethy Bridge and Glen More via Ryvoan. The road was to be nine miles and it would be *"advantageous to winter sport interests in Grantown on Spey"*. It was considered useful to have a new road from Tomintoul to Crathie on Deeside. The route was to be from Tomintoul via Delnabo, Inchrory and Loch Builg and by-passing the often snow blocked Lecht road down to Corgarff.

Then there was a study to connect Blair Atholl with the proposed road *route linking Deeside to Speyside by way of Glen Feshie. That plan was, "to link the Ben Lawers skiing area in Perthshire and, together with a new road across the Moor of Rannoch, that of Glencoe, with Deeside. The costs of the foregoing four roads cannot be estimated with any precision. On the basis of being single track roads with passing places it is not likely to be less than £2.6 million."*

That was in 1967 and having studied the feasibility of criss-crossing the entire central area of the Cairngorms with new roads, the planners then went into hibernation for many years. In 1973 the Inverness County Architects Office recommended that official backing be given to a snow survey of the Aonach Mor region of Ben Nevis. In presenting the proposal, the County Architect, Douglas Calder stated that the planning committee should think in terms of having a new ski centre in that area within the next five years. That was in 1973 and it was 1989 before that particular development took shape and then that only happened because of the persistence of one man, Ian Sykes with some venture capital input and grant aid.

Inverness Roads Committee also agreed to make a detailed feasibility study of the proposed Glen Feshie road project. The £40,000 costs of that study were to be shared with Aberdeenshire County Council and it was planned that the study would start in the spring, taking six months to complete. The proposed Glen Feshie road was originally surveyed by General Wade's engineers in the years before the 1745-46 rebellion. Instead of being used to facilitate the pacification of the Highlands, the proposed new road in 1973 was seen as an essential link for the growing commercial, timber and tourist trades between east and west and a first step to the development of Braemar and the Ben a Bhuird regions, for skiing. Development was in the air, grand ideas were being floated and some were being swept along in the excitement. But, even then, I thought the proposed Glen Feshie road and other roads, were farfetched, a step too far.

Ben Wyvis

As the boom times progressed, others were looking at new sites for possible development. Cairngorm, Glencoe and Glenshee/Glen Clunie were all firmly established and turning over profits as the numbers of customers increased year on year. Near Braemar, the Mar Lodge project tried but failed in what I termed glorious failure. In the north, a small number of local skiers had traditionally reported good snow holding slopes in Easter Ross on the eastern slopes of Ben Wyvis. The mountain dominates the sky line from

Inverness and Dingwall and a group of hoteliers, business people and councillors initiated an investigation into the potential of the area.

Ben Wyvis Ski Development: Report of Investigations 1966/67 and 1967/68.

"The main work took the form of weekly surveys to assess the state of the snow, backed up by comprehensive weather records; and of a preliminary engineering survey of an access line. The first year's work proved most encouraging and the Ben Wyvis Ski Development Association pushed ahead with the other parts of the project to assess the development prospects for a winter sports centre. The engineering survey identified the line of an access road to the bottom of the proposed ski area with a length of four and three quarter miles while the building of the proposed chairlift in a sheltered position would be straightforward.

Four distinct ski runs or snowfields existed with a variety of grades suitable for moderate and skilled skiers. These runs were measured as being 900 ft, 700 ft, 1,050 ft. in vertical descent. For durability in a winter which was milder than usual, these natural runs compared favourably with the developed runs with snow fencing, at Cairngorm and Glenshee. Simple snow-fencing and similar work would extend and render more durable, several of the runs. There were additional areas of snow with suitable slopes available for nursery skiers, apart from runs on other parts of the mountain which might be utilised at a later stage.

The high winds from west and north which during the winter of 1966/67 interrupted chairlift operation frequently on Cairngorm and at times even drove skiers off parts of the slopes, were found to be almost wholly excluded from the Ben Wyvis slopes by the shelter given by the main ridge to the north-west and the spur to the north-east.

The whole of the area for early development is in one ownership, that of the Forestry Commission, although there are privately held sporting rights. The summit ridge is a quite outstanding viewpoint with views in clear weather over almost the whole of the northern mainland of Ross-shire and Sutherland as well over the Moray Firth. Access to it in the summer time would prove to be a great attraction to the many bus touring parties and other visitors.

The survey work was continued into a second year with financial funding by the Scottish Tourist Board. While the weather pattern in the second year proved to be different, it proved that Ben Wyvis was an early skiing hill in that it did not need much depth of snow for the slopes to be skiable. The hill is almost entirely covered in grass with few rocks and rough ground, whereas at the main Scottish centre, Cairngorm, there has to be either a heavy snow fall or heavy drifting into the gullies and corries to fill the very rough terrain sufficiently, before skiing is possible. This could be an important factor when commercially developed, in years when snow is scarce over the Christmas season. It was in the second season of the survey that the Highlands and Islands Development Board took an interest by providing a Snowtrac vehicle for more regular observations of the mountain."

Ski fever was spreading like wild fire and eyes were being cast on every potential mountain. Even in 2010, further tentative questions were being asked about the feasibility of modified ski developments on Ben Wyvis.

Politicians Change Horses

It was only when the conservation lobby began to be really active in the early 1980s that the Scottish Office came to life again. Instead of looking at any of their own, less radical original plans, proposing new developments at existing ski centres, they totally switched all allegiances and fell over themselves to be nice to the environmentalists. It was a turnabout on a major scale but the politicians were getting the message from the vociferous green lobbyists, and for them, votes were what counted.

Ironically, in 1973 George Younger, the Scottish Under Secretary for Development spoke to the Annual Gathering of Scottish Ski Clubs and said, *"In the past, development plans have done little more than catalogue possible land uses. Authorities did not always carry out detailed research into the feasibility of such land use and sometimes the proposals smacked more of hope than reality. The new authorities* (this was 1973 when new regional and local government structures were coming into being) *will be required to prepare structure plans which will have to cater for recreation. Government is acutely aware of the importance of recreation in their efforts to attract industry and investment to Scotland. The expansion of skiing is a positive factor in attracting industry and employment."*

Mr. Younger then went on to praise the Scottish Tourist Board and the Highlands and Islands Development Board in giving substantial funding for the new Coire na Ciste lifts. He spoke too, of his £60 million five year plan to reconstruct the A9 Perth to Inverness road. Today, only short stretches of dual carriageway have been created.. The result is that road fatalities are still frequent and the pressure to dual the entire A9 is constantly on the agenda at Holyrood.

Chapter 19

Doctors on call

Assorted Problems

On the west side of the Cairngorms there were boom times and all the facilities were being stretched. Hotels were crowded, bed and breakfast houses did roaring trade. So too were the rescue and medical services. Dr. Neil Macdonald the well known Aviemore medic was kept busy dealing with skiing accidents and the ambulance service was kept busy carrying his referrals of more serious ski injuries to hospital in Grantown on Spey or Inverness.

He observed in 1987 that about 60% of the clients he and his two colleagues were treating were results of skiers colliding or injuring themselves by trying to avoid collisions. He knew that before, when the slopes were less crowded, injuries tended to be sprained or broken legs or ankles but he was then having to deal with injuries to the upper body, such as fractured arms, chest damage and concussion. He later said, *"There is no doubt in my mind that these injuries are being caused by the overcrowding on the mountain. I call them "conservation" accidents. If the Conservationists who are opposed to further development of skiing on Cairngorm would let skiers have a little more room then I am certain the numbers of accidents would drop."*

In the beginning, the classic skiing accident was the broken ankle but with the advent of higher and stiffer boots the syndrome virtually disappeared to be replaced by the more serious twisting fracture of the mid leg and then of course there has always been the "Knackered Knee" problem. Good release bindings coupled with better education about how to adjust them made life a bit safer. Except of course when dangers lie in having super efficient bindings which eject the skier at speed and at the first hint of a fall. You can take your pick; you can have a dislocated shoulder, a broken collar bone, broken upper arms or you can fracture one or more of half a dozen bones in the lower arm or the hand.

Yet another condition which hit the pages of the British Medical Journal in the 1980s and stemmed from the pen of an Oxford medical consultant, was the "Moon Boot Syndrome". He had personally suffered from the problem as did his children and he described the symptoms in gruesome detail. After wearing the boots during a particularly long journey back from the Alps, they found their feet swollen, the soles white, wrinkled and very tender. Standing was painful with the sensation of standing on a course cheese grater. The syndrome superficially resembled Trench Foot and Water Immersion Syndrome all experienced by men in the trenches of the First World War and even in the Falklands Campaign.

Bristle Bum

There are other conditions associated with skiing on the many artificial ski slopes. Take for instance the Hillend Thumb, the condition which so easily follows a fall on the bristle mats of the slope. An unprotected thumb so easily gets caught in the plastic mesh foundation and all users are required to wear gloves. In England, the Rossendale Bristle Bum is easily recognised as a red rash or series of petechial haemorrhages on the fleshy cheeks of the backside. The condition is readily seen among novice skiers who tend to "sit down" frequently. The list of possible ski injuries is long and there were fatalities.

Back on Cairngorm, the rescue team leader, Neil Baxter, and his squad of nine had to deal with up to 30 accidents each day in high season. He said, *"Before, it always used to be at Christmas, half-term and Easter. Now it's going like a fair, seven days a week".* Tom Paul at that time the assistant general manager to Bob Clyde said in print, *"We have reached saturation point. People are getting into the car parks at 8am in order to get a place. Every year the numbers wanting to ski the mountain are getting bigger and bigger. But, we simply cannot move because of the opposition which is put up to any expansion we propose ... skiing is a successful and vital Highland industry built on the enthusiasm of skiers in Scotland."*

The immediate response from Mrs. Pat Wells, convenor of Badenoch and Strathspey Conservation Group was, *"The main reasons for the number of accidents are unrelated to conservation issues ... they are due to over-publicity and over-glamorisation of the facilities at Cairngorm, sub-arctic weather and poor snow conditions, physically unfit or tired skiers, failure of the Cairngorm Chairlift Co, to limit the number of skiers to a figure compatible with safety in prevailing conditions, and bad policing of the slopes which result in novices attempting difficult slopes, running out of control and crashing into others."*

Now, that is one of the longest single sentences I have ever had to type out and, if you run through it again you will see that it is obvious the increase in skiing injuries was all the fault of those awful Chairlift people, the unfitness of skiers in general, the poor weather conditions, too much publicity and etc.,etc. As they say in the Doric: *"It wis a'bodies fault bit Bella's."* My observation was that there was little attempt to publicise Scottish skiing and no one ever thought it was a glamorous sport. Skiing just happened, and it was an unstoppable movement. Mrs. Wells is still an active campaigner. This time it is to disapprove of wind turbines.

Glenshee First Aid

On the topic of medical assistance at the ski slopes, this became very necessary from the beginning. In the early days, the ski club buses carried basic first aid equipment such as splints and bandages to stabilise broken bones. But as soon as the ski centres opened up and numbers increased, they were obliged to provide first aid rooms and trained staff for the inevitable injuries. Bumps and bruises, cuts and abrasions were frequent and then of course, the classic broken ankles.

The Scout Movement played a huge part in the establishment of the first aid and search and rescue services at Glenshee, and it was highly rated. From the beginning, the team was manned by Rover Scouts, the forerunners of today's Venture Scouts and Dr Paul Mackenzie and Dr Swanston, a retired medic from Kirkcaldy provided the professional back up. The Doc was a ken-speckle figure well known on the hill but he hit the headlines for all the wrong reasons. He was on duty and watching one race, starting from the top of the Tiger Piste. The run, when the snow is in good condition, is challenging but, when it is icy, as it frequently was, it was more than challenging and became formidable.

The profile of the hill is convex at the top half, when ideal slopes tend to be concave. The slope that day was very icy and even the top competitors were having difficulty in holding an edge. The "Doc" did lose an edge that day and rattled down some 300ft. suffering abrasions and cuts to the head. His own team were to hand and he was carted off to hospital. All in a day's work.

Commissioner Ian Jones of the Scout Association said in 1980, when congratulating the team, that while the incidence of leg fractures have diminished dramatically there were many other accidents to be dealt which including one, where a customer for first aid staggered into the medical room complaining of foot pains and that he was constantly falling over on the slopes. It turned out that he had his boots on the wrong feet!

Trade was brisk and statistics showed that in the 1968 season, 198 injured skiers were treated at the first aid room. There were 68 stretcher cases moved off the hill by the Rover Scouts, 46 ambulance journeys to hospitals and sundry minor injuries.

Benighted

Occasionally, a helicopter was called to evacuate more serious injuries and, on one memorable weekend, trapped skiers. It was January 1988 and it was one of those dangerous storms that sweep in from the south west and on that occasion it caught out the Glenshee operators and the police because of the speed and ferocity of the blizzard. Around 1800 skiers were trapped overnight in the area when the police deemed it necessary to close both routes, north and south of the A93, for public safety. Road chaos followed and everyone was benighted

All the buildings, the ski school building, the shop, the Scottish Ski Club hut and the house above the main centre building occupied by David Patterson the centre manager and his family were used to shelter the multitude for almost 24 hours and only a few with special medical needs were evacuated by helicopter. There were no fatalities, just an uncomfortable night for already tired skiers. Thereafter, the police and the chairlift company tightened up safety procedures to speed the progressive shut down of lifts and tows and the evacuation of the slopes when storm conditions swept in.

Sudden storms caused chaos and severe problems for the snow clearing services from time to time but "stupid" drivers were also a problem. The senior executive of Grampian Region, Mr. Douglas Macnaughton was critical about the organisation at the ski centre but especially at the conduct of some drivers. When the blizzard blew in it turned out to be far worse than expected and the ski centre progressively closed down all the lifts. Meanwhile the snow gates at the foot of the hills at Braemar and at Spittal of Glenshee were closed to stop further attempts by cars to continue uphill. Lack of information caused some skiers up at the ski centre who heard that the road had closed, to attempt to leave, but many cars stuck in drifting snow and blocked the whole road, north and south. Mr. Macnaughton was reported as saying, *"We could send up a large snow cutter blower, but it can't chew its way through abandoned motor cars."*

The result that weekend was that 1800 were trapped at Glenshee, some at the Lecht and also 300 motorists were trapped on the A9 in five miles of drifts, four trains became snow-bound and three climbers died in the Cairngorms. No skiers perished on that occasion.

To say that emergency services were stretched, was a gross understatement for there were 1000 square kilometres of Grampian Region without electricity which needed priority road clearing. The Glenshee Centre coped remarkable well with the stranded skiers to be sheltered and sustained overnight. Subsequently, the entire system of communication between all the services and the centre were overhauled. Snow gates at the ski centre at the top of the hill pass on the A 93 were fitted to stop snow ploughs being hindered by snow-blocked and broken down cars and systems to coordinate all services were introduced. One difficulty identified had been that radio communications in Glenshee were not always perfect.

The Police blasted some maverick and thoughtless motorists who, *"manhandled the snow gates off their hinges or squeezed their cars over a footpath at the side of a locked gate"*. The police had a problem in enforcing the shutting of the road because it was a through road and people had a right to use it. Shortly after, when a Bill went through Parliament, it became an offence to interfere with snow gates.

Ouch

Morphine is a great comfort for those with painful injuries but it's use was always well controlled. My own flirtation with the proscribed drug came one day on Meall Odhar when our group was heather hopping. I took a tumble and tore ligaments in a knee. A good friend carried me on his back for half a mile to the Dundee Ski Club hut where another friend and club member, Dr. George Lumsden of Peterhead gave me a shot of morphine before the long sledge trip down to the A93. It's wonderful stuff morphine, for a photograph revealed that I was grinning widely while being sledged off the hill.

Then of course, the more comical injuries, sometimes self inflicted, which enlivened the ski buses travellers. *"It was towards the end of a good day on the hills at Abergeldie. It was high season with abundant snow and, a tractor tow which was well tuned and working overtime. On his last run down to the road and the homeward bound club bus, one of the tow team workers had tucked a quarter bottle of whisky in his rear pocket. It was flat and fitted comfortably, until that is, he fell on his bottom and heard a crunch followed by pain in his buttock region.*

He dribbled whisky and blood until we got him onto the bus, where we laid him face down on the back seat while we administered first aid. Now the buttocks tend to bleed freely, so he was told to lie still and behave himself. The bus stopped at a well known watering hole on the way home and a medical student gave the patient strict orders to lie still or he would bleed to death, while all the rest headed for the bar. The bit about possible death if he moved was all a hoax of course but it was a punishment for being so careless with that lovely wee bottle. We believe he carries the scar on his backside to this day."

Drunk in Charge

Alcohol on the ski slopes became an issue in 1970 when some European countries became concerned about drunken skiers and the accidents they could cause. The subject was raised at national level in Scotland but was greeted with derision and the inevitable question, "how would they catch the offenders?". In Austria it was blood-test level for drivers in some countries. Austria had professional Piste Police who were pretty hot on catching speeding and dangerous skiers and taking the ski pass away from them.

Guy Chilver-Stainer the Secretary to the Scottish National Ski Council, was quoted by the Daily Express as saying, *"I don't consider it would be a problem. Scotland is renowned for conviviality but not on a mountain. Drinking is usually reserved for "apres ski". In the Alps one can be technically sober at ground level but by the time you reach altitude at say 10,000 ft. you can be drunk with the effects of altitude. I have seen it happen and it's hilarious. Even the best skiers can fall about from time to time."*

Which reminds me that I once skied around the Porte du Soleil with a group of hard skiers, one of whom carried a pair of hollow ski poles or drinking sticks. The left one was filled with Poire William liqueur and the right stick had Gin and Tonic, heavy on the gin and light on the other! Now, each ski pole carried half a pint and at frequent stops the sticks were passed around our group of five. The ski poles were empty by lunchtime and were refilled … every day for a week. The stops became more frequent and there was much "bon ami". The skiing was pretty good too.

On a more serious note, over many years the average death toll on the Scottish mountains each year was around 22 to 24, mainly among the climbing fraternity. When skiing burst on the scene and thousands more began to go up into the winter mountains, the prophets of doom said that many more would fall off their chairlifts and ski off to die in the sub-arctic conditions, like lemmings. They were wrong of course for the number of winter fatalities hardly increased. Accidents did happen and when Jack Frost struck, the injury rate increased. It was mainly bruising and lacerations from falls on icy pistes. But deaths did occur as in Corrie na Ciste in 1991 when a 20 year old miner from Alva in Clackmannan, lost control on the steep and icy West Wall. The area had been closed off by the Chairlift Company but the man and three companions ignored the warning.

Chapter 20

True Grit

Inuit Vocabulary

Each season in Scotland brought different challenges. One winter we had the "Year of the Stones" when all the pistes in Scotland were thin and bare and definitely "gritty", when great gouges appeared on the ski soles of even the most careful skiers. Then we had the "Ice Winters", before there were efficient machines which could groom the pistes before the night frosts could turn them to boiler plate sheet ice. These machines cost a lot of money and few centres could afford them in the early days. Cairngorm just twenty years ago paid £90,000 for a new Kassbohrer machine. Then there were the many "windy winters", when the gales always seem to blow hardest at weekends when most skiers were attempting to ski and many events had to be cancelled or re-scheduled as lifts and tows were closed down.

Skier days at the ski centres dropped dramatically in winter 1967 and from a possible 90 days from 1st January the Cairngorm upper section chairlift was only able to operate for nine days. The weather men at the Climatological Service Office in Edinburgh went on record as saying, "This has been the worst spell of consistently high winds for 40 years". The anemometer situated on pylon number seven on the upper White Lady chair, recorded automatically, the wind speeds and direction on the exposed ridge of the mountain. This was recorded in the manager's office and information boards told the customers why lifts were not working. At the beginning of March, the wind recorder marked up the incredible speed of 143 mph. And at that time it was ratified as a record wind speed for the

British Isles. And still, some skiers attempted to ski on the lower slopes that day! Addiction leads people to do crazy things!

They say that the Inuit peoples of Greenland have forty different words in their language, to describe the many types of snow they have to live with. I would suggest that the early Scottish skiers could come up with as many and more, richly descriptive words: Porridge, slush, spring snow, ice, rippled ice, lumpy ice, boiler plate ice, snow crusted heather, ice crusted heather, corrugated ice, muddy snow, muddy slush, lethal ice, sticky snow, wet snow, very wet snow, more slush, spin drifted snow, crud, breakable crust, rocks and big rocks. And, all that, even before the obscenities began.

Finally, on occasions … fresh powder snow, blue sky, windless conditions with glimpses of Nirvana.

Spin-drift, by the way is when high winds carry lying snow across the surface of the hill, up to perhaps knee level. One can only ski slowly in these conditions but, as soon as one stops and because you can't see where your feet are or where the ground level is, you simply fall over as you stand still. It's a strange sensation. I wonder if the Inuits have a word for that?

Winter Olympic Weather

But is it actually true that Scotland's weather is so bad? True we have high winds, and snow shortages and blizzards and rapid snow thaws and everything else that nature can throw at us. But, so have ski mountains all across the world. The facts are, that wherever skiing takes place, wherever the International Olympic Committee chooses to hold the Winter Olympics every four years, the elements conspire to halt the action. Take the example of Sapporo in Japan in 1972.

Scots took part at the Winter Games that year and BASI sent a demonstration team of ski instructors which was highly acclaimed. Just a few days before the competitions began, the Japanese hosts were hugely embarrassed to see torrential rain and an unseasonable thaw set in. It was hailed as an unavoidable fact that all Winter Olympics over the previous fifty

A poor spring

years since the Winter Games had been added as an Olympic Festival, bad weather had intervened. It was thought by the traditionalists, that Zeus and the other ancient Greek gods atop Mount Olympus, were showing their disapproval that winter sport had been added to the ancient Greek summer festival. Or was it Avery Brundage's final words of disapproval about winter sports becoming an Olympic sport?

As soon as Winter Olympics were planned, the dates were set and athletes arrived, things happened to disrupt the Games. It became too hot or too cold. There was too much snow or too little. In Grenoble in 1968, rain washed away the ice on the bob run to cancel preparations, but came down as snow on a different mountain in such quantities as to cancel all practice downhill ski runs. After the formal competitions began, a thaw caused postponement of toboggan competition while winds and fog temporarily cancelled the alpine races.

That was the year Jean-Claud Killy won his third Olympic title. The Norwegians claimed to have the perfect conditions for competitions and boasted about Oslo as the venue. In 1952 they produced the charts and statistics to prove their point. Just a week before the Games were due to begin gales removed all the snow around Oslo and the Holmenkollen main skiing site. Embarrassed officials had to close all practice venues and the Norwegian Army were called in to truck in snow from higher regions. Just two days before the opening ceremony, the snow arrived and national honour was saved.

Squaw Valley in California was awarded the Winter Games in 1960 because it was reputed to have average annual snow falls of 37 feet. Two weeks before the opening ceremony, torrential rain and 100 mile gales stripped away all the snow. Providentially, more snow arrived just in time to save the Games. I could go on and on to bore you with tales about how fickle the weather gods can be. I am just making the point that Scottish winter weather is not too untypical. When it is good it can be very good. When it is bad it can be bl***y awful. And just to underline my point, in 1932 the Winter Games were held in Lake Placid, again in the US, during a mountain heat wave. The speed skaters competed in slush and were likened to water skiers. That year was the warmest winter in Lake Placid's history. Four years later the Games went to Garmisch-Partenkirchen, in Bavaria, during Hitler's triumphant years. In keeping with the Olympic tradition, the German winter resort had neither snow nor frost. On the opening day, a blizzard arrived, simultaneously with the arrival of the Fuhrer!

Chapter 21

Big Time Politics

Amateur V Professional

My own meeting with Sir Arnold Lunn came when a team of Scottish race officials were invited by Helen Tomkinson of the Kandahar Club to officiate at the Kandahar Martini International Citadin events to be held in Murren, Switzerland in 1969. It was only then that I became aware of the fierce political battles being waged between the International Olympic Committee and the Federation International de Ski {F.I.S]. Avery Brundage was the legendary president of the I.O.C who reigned supreme for too long and frequently rode roughshod over his many committees and sub-committees. He was adamant that all Olympic sport must be amateur, even while the movement towards loosening the rules was gaining ground. All sports were flirting with professionalism covertly but, American born Brundage was adamant about his ruling that only "pure" sportsmanship would do.

The crunch came when he barred Austrian Karl Schranz from racing at the Sapporo Winter Olympics in Japan in 1972. Schranz was the world successor to Claude Killy of France and won 20 major downhill events. The reason for barring him? *"considering the activity and the influence of Schranz in the field of international skiing, and in the manner in which he has permitted the use of his photograph and his name in commercial advertising, he is declared ineligible to take part in the eleventh Winter Games".* Many of Schranz's closest rivals were upset by the ruling for they were all guilty of "professionalism" at some level.

A black list compiled by Brundage alleged to contain the names of between 30 and 40 skiers breaking his rules. France's World Cup winner Henri Duvillard said, *"They wanted a head and they chose Karl."* There was a fierce reaction as Austria threatened to withdraw its complete ski team and there was rumour of total withdrawal of ski sport, with the threat of the World Cup ski circuits becoming the most important forum for downhill skiing. Some say it is today.

Avery Brundage continued to rule the IOC with his autocratic fist and before 1972 when he handed over his fiefdom to Lord Killanin of Ireland he threatened to drop the Winter Olympics as being unrepresentative of the Olympic ideal of being "professional" and the "puppets" of commercial interests. The problem had smouldered for many years and in the UK earlier attempts had been made by the then Sports Minister who sent a memorandum to all National Governing bodies in sport. It was a plea that all sports should work towards the progressive elimination of the terms, "amateur and professional" This was a direct attack on the Olympic definition which at that time was the cause of so many of the anomalies and abuses.

On a different plane entirely and well before the Olympic confrontation, the Scottish Racing Clubs in 1965 altered the hitherto strict ruling on amateurism and professionalism by allowing certain categories of instructor to race on the Scottish racing circuits. Immediately, many fine continental professional instructors became eligible and in one season alone, the standard of racing across the country improved in all groups.

Karl Schranz raced on Cairngorm at one British International at the end of his world cup season, as did several world class skiers. At the time Schranz described his philosophy, *"If Mr Brundage had been as poor as I was and many other athletes, I wonder if he would not have a different attitude. The ideal Olympics would be one with no discrimination whatever regarding race, colour of a man's skin, his religion or politics, whether he was rich or poor. If we followed Mr. Brundage's recommendations to their true end, then the Olympics would be a competition for the very rich. No man of ordinary means could ever afford to excel in his sport".*

Hypocrisy

Shamateurism was rife with some nations employing athletes in jobs which allowed them to train full time and Russia and East Germany were blatant in supporting their top athletes. At the Winter Games, Austria and France were also guilty and the USA had a system of sporting scholarships at its universities which also allowed athletes to concentrate principally on their chosen sports. The French press became very agitated about Avery Brundage, the President of the International Olympic Committee in 1968, for his attempts to keep the Games "pure" and amateur.

The newspaper France-Soir said that within 20 years, winter sports had become a huge industry and that none of that pleased the *"fine gentlemen of the International Olympic Committee. Its president Mr Avery Brundage, wears his 80 years lightly, is an American gentleman, a billionaire who collects Chinese and Japanese objects d'art. Count Jean de Beaumont is a banker and the best gun in France. Lord Killanin, an Irish aristocrat, seems to have stepped out of a novel by Dickens. All would like to keep sport, "pure, honest and disinterested. " It is only necessary to go and see in the chalets of Chamrousse, the skiing champions, to realise that there is a tragic gulf between the fine gentlemen of the hotels of Grenoble and these boys that go to the mines. These sons of peasants and small inn keepers certainly reckon that their success will bring them fame and fortune."*

The left-wing newspaper "Combat" wrote that Brundage had waited until the last moment to oppose a practice which was not new. It added, *"Let not one present those champions as amateurs and let the Olympic oath remain in the dressing rooms. Sport should be the last domain in which hypocrisy has pride of place".*

Brundage adopted a dignified position of principle by emphasizing, without comment, that he would not personally present medals to the Alpine skiers. When he did present medals to the hockey players and skaters he was booed in the ice stadium. The world of sport has moved on and professionalism is taken for granted. But, has big money crept into sport at many levels, to its detriment? It is tempting to follow that train of thought, but not now.

L to R. Lt.General Reggie Leathes and Maria Goldberger from the London
Establishment, Lewis Drysdale and the author at the British Championships on
Cairngorm.1972.

Clouding the Issue

The traditional alpine bases of the Downhill Ski Club [DHO] in Wengen
and the Kandahar Club in Murren, were where youth training, had taken
place by tradition and continued for many years. Helen Tomkinson,
Elizabeth Hussey and Maria Goldberger, the "Grande Dames" of the
Kandahar Club and the British Ladies Ski Club were hugely influential in
their time by sitting on various F.I.S. international committees.

In London, politics were clouding the main issues, again. The Ski Club
of Great Britain founded in 1907 felt aggrieved because, *"The established
prestige and position of the SCGB., which has been justly earned over a long
period and which are the basis of the influence which the Club has in skiing
affairs, are apparently being undermined."* Their concern was about the

relationship between the SCGB and the newly formed National Ski Federation of Great Britain.

The NSFGB was formed in 1964, ostensibly to raise funds and manage the British Teams, but within a few years had run into financial difficulties, expecting all the G.B. clubs to bail it out. It became a bit of a dog fight with the SCGB which claimed that with its long traditions and history, it had been accepted, both at home and abroad, as the "National Club". It was aggrieved that the NSFGB was not prepared to defer to and treat the SCGB accordingly. In addition they were puzzled perhaps by the astonishing progress of the sport in Scotland.

Helen Tomkinson was the first to come to Scotland to see for herself what was happening and later, she took the Kandahar Martini International races to Scotland. But before that she invited a team of eight Scottish race officials to assist with the Martini Kandahar Race meeting being held in Murren in Switzerland in 1969. It was an exciting opportunity of course, but we had to work hard.

The team consisted of five from the Highland Ski Club, Bob Ritchie, Bill Garland, Frank Allan, Jim Kelman and Bob Hannant. Two came from the Aberdeen Club, Stuart Wilson and myself, and from the Scottish Club came Ken Armstrong from Edinburgh. We found our own way out to Murren, but from then on, we were looked after by the Kandahar Club. Murren still had many strong British connections, established in a bye gone era. Access from the valley was only by cog railway and there were no cars in the village. There was still a feeling of old Victorian elegance, with some of the large hotels having been built in that era. We were housed in a very old wooden chalet on the main street called Chalet Fontana, leased annually by the "K" Club for its members and junior training squads.

Too Many Cooks

The slope selected for the international slalom event was steep, too steep for the under powered piste machine of the time to cope with and so we and the

Kandahar officials linked arms and stamped down the slope, repeatedly, to create a firm base for the course. Leading the team was Helen Tomkinson, into her 60's and full of energy.

Bob Ritchie of the "Highland", was leader of the Cairngorm Timing Unit at home and he took over that job in Murren. He literally straightened out the professional but lackadaisical Longine timing team sent from Geneva for the races, and took charge. The race organisation was somewhat chaotic and we Scots derived some scraps of comfort from the knowledge that our systems at home were better. The main problem was undoubtedly the number of cooks ... there were too many!

For instance, the appointed course setter marked out the course and left us to piste and prepare it manually. The head of the local Ski School came along and moved some poles, so we shovelled some more and swore a little. Then the Chief of the Race made a few more suggestions and alterations were made and, we swore a little more loudly. Then the top Swiss dignitary for the whole international event came along and put in his tupence worth. Now, in Scotland the volunteer helpers would not have stood for all that nonsense. Despite all the fuss, the courses were set, the races started on time and, there was no cock-up with the timing! It was an International Citadin Race with 12 nations competing and the principal sponsor was Martini.

Chapter 22

Virgin Ski Tracks

First Down

After a spell when the pistes were tired, icy perhaps and bare in places, a heavy fall of snow overnight was greeted with such joy and excitement. The early birds would be up early, checking the forecast for the day and driving like mad to be first up the mountain and first on the lifts and tows. "Older" skiers will know what I am talking about when I say that it is another sort of addiction. A dream, to be the first to ski down, even the little Hayfield slope at the foot of the Cairngorm Ski Road by Glenmore when the upper road was closed or even before the road existed. Or, the first to ski down the Corrie na Ciste or the White Lady on Cairngorm or the Tiger Piste at Glenshee, after a heavy fall of snow. If you were among first on the hill on such Cairngorm occasions you might have caught a glimpse of Mr Robert Clyde, MBE., General Manager, Cairngorm Chairlift Company skiing on his own domain ... "before the punters arrived".

It is much the same in the Alps. However early you are in Val Thorens or Val d'Isere, the highest resorts in France, someone will have been first to make tracks on the new snow. I am convinced that a degree of bribery must take place between chairlift operators and those shadowy figures who leave their early morning tracks on the virgin snow, even before the lifts officially open to the public.

Touching the void

My first real experience of virgin snow fields on a vast scale was during a

Below Mont Blanc

press trip to Cervinia in the Italian Alps. It was early February and the snow slopes under the Matterhorn, that most photographed of mountains, were near perfect. We had almost skied out that resort, when we were told that the classic ski run from Italy into Chamonix in France had been closed for ten days because of blizzards but was to open the following morning. It was the famous eighteen kilometre glacier run called the Vallee Blanche or sometimes the Mer du Glace. An American journalist and I, opted to grab the chance and arranged an early start with a guide. Driving through Courmayeur we were the first to take the early cable car up to Helbronner, the top station on the Italian side of Mont Blanc massif and the frontier.

We had a flat kilometre of deep snow to plod across to reach the top of the glacier. From then on it was sheer exhilaration with more than a touch of fear. We ran the first downhill section before reaching a steep section where the glacier ice had developed huge ripples and deep crevasses, many covered by nearly two metres of new snow. The guide went ahead to make tracks and check for dangerous snow bridge crossings.

I had never encountered Italian ski guides before and was surprised to see how laid back he was during this tense time on the descent. We skied very close to deep, blue ice crevasses and witnessed one or two collapsing snow bridges within a metre or two of our tracks. Our guide tended to ski ahead of us and to take quick swigs of Grappa, an Italian fire water … not too reassuring for our small group! I just hoped that he would have a long enough rope to pull me out, if I suddenly disappeared down into the icy blue depths. I admit to having an vivid imagination and I had just read Joe Simpson's book "Touching the Void".

Then, the glorious bit! The deep blue crevasses behind us, we had snow, deep and even, stretching downhill for many kilometres. On all sides were

In the Vallee Blanche

the incredible peaks and towers of the region, seen for the first time up close and dreamt about and, ours were virgin ski tracks. The long powder run completed, we then had a stiff climb to get above the treacherous ice falls at the very foot of the glacier. Then the long, long forest tracks sweeping right down and into the town of Chamonix itself. Wow, what an experience! Nothing quite like it in Scotland.

Pecking Order

Having first been a climber before catching the skiing bug, I had to admit to being a bit of a snob at times. In the early climbing fraternity, we pigeon-holed everyone else mainly by the clothes they wore, starting with the lowly walkers and trippers with woolly bobble hats and inappropriate boots. Then there were the "ham and eggers" who, at the campsites or bothies cooked bacon and eggs for a leisurely breakfast, while we had a "jammie" piece and a quick cup of tea, in our rush to get up onto the hill. We also frowned at those with ostentatious new gear, or had girls with them. We were the boys; we wore ex-army kit and we had clinkers and muggers, climbing nails, knocked into the soles of our leather soled climbing boots, before the wonderful commando rubber soles became available. But, at the top of the heap were the real climbers, the post war "Aberdeen Boys".

They were a group of young men, my generation, in the North East in the late 1940s and early 1950s who were pioneers in rock and ice climbing. They picked up from the pre-war men who had made some of the first ascents in the Scottish mountains and whose names went into the early Scottish Mountaineering Club Journals. But, the "Aberdeen Boys" were the first of a new wave of talented climbers who opened up rock and ice climbs in post war Scotland.

Successive S.M.C. Journals gave descriptions and acknowledgements of their first assents. Bill Brooker, Mac Smith, John Morgan, the Tewnion brothers and Kenny Winram, made many first ascents and we knew most of them by sharing bothy space, seeing them about the hills and sharing the climber's buses. We got to know many of them in later life because of shared interests, but at the time, in the mountaineers pecking order, my group would have been rated second or third. Which brings to mind that wonderful television sketch with John Cleese, Ronnie Barker and Ronnie Corbett about pecking orders and the class system. Cleese said, "I'm upper class and I look down on him." Barker said, "I'm middle class and I look down on him." Corbett said, "I'm working class and I look up to them." Transferred into climbing parlance, as I say, we were second or third class and we looked up to them.

My little group of serious hill walkers and advanced scramblers, was climbing during the same era as the "Aberdeen Boys". If we did happen to climb any of the "classified" routes, it was purely by accident, because we did not aspire to own copies of the Scottish Mountaineering Club Guide books. Lochnagar was our territory for it was accessible and it was surrounded by bothies. Robertson's stable at the Spittal of Glen Muick, Lochend bothy at the north end of Loch Muick, the Gelder cottage and stables above Balmoral Castle and, stables at Loch Callater and close to Braemar. Sadly all these have been vandalised, demolished or closed.

Lochnagar also took its toll of young lives in the period up to the mid 1960s. Two in particular were known to me. Bill Stewart died in the corrie in 1953 and I had travelled with him in the Aberdeen contingent of Scouts selected to attend the 1947 World Peace Scout Jamboree at Moison near Paris. Later, in 1961, Ronnie Sellers fell and was killed on the Parallel Buttress "B" when his belay on a loose rock came away and pulled him down. He was Secretary of the Etchecan Climbing Club in the years I was Chairman of the Aberdeen Ski Club and we organised joint club events.

Snobs

Skiers also have a pecking order and I, also being an inverted snob, just can't help myself when being overtaken by an elegant mover who curves and weaves down the mountain in complete and effortless control. I automatically hate him, or her, because they make me feel inadequate. Kenny Dickson, an Aviemore instructor used to ski so eloquently and rhythmically as he skied the White Lady, while plugged in to his Sony Walkman, playing Samba music. His was the first such music machine on the mountain and samba music has for ever for me, been so exotic.

Rare Breeds

My time for feeling superior came in the late 1940s, early 50's when I would stagger off the Strachan's Deeside bus at 10.30 on a Sunday night. It was the last "climbers bus" from Braemar and Ballater and it was invariably full of rucsacs and booted climbers. My route home in Aberdeen was to walk down Union Street in the town centre, for 500yds to catch my home bus. In common with the times, many young men and girls used to perambulate up and down town centres, talking, flirting and gossiping.

In Aberdeen it was called "Walking the Mat", the three quarter mile length of Union Street and it had been the custom for a hundred years or more. My Grandmother no doubt met my Grandfather there, one Sunday evening. Even in my day there were no pubs open on Sundays, no cinemas, no coffee shops, no television, few motor cars and the buses and trams stopped at 10.45pm. A friend of mine wrote the definitive history of "Walking the Mat" and I have that book in my collection.

We few eccentrics would appear with muddy boots and climbing ropes and big packs, so naturally we became the butt of humour. I had many cat-calls before I got home. But, I did feel superior, for I was a climber! Well, perhaps just a very keen hill walker and an enthusiastic scrambler. But, when I began to carry skis and they were 220 cm long and I had to struggle to load them onto a corporation bus or a tram, I felt even more superior, for we were a rare breed!

Chapter 23

Lurcher's Gully

A Political Battle Field

The ski lift companies were constantly under pressure to enlarge and improve facilities, witness the letters of complaints they received about the length of lift queues and the dangers of congestion. The project then became the hot potato for a decade. Mr Michael Forsythe the then Scottish Secretary in pre-devolution Scotland was as indecisive as we expect our politicians to be. His public inquiries were unclear, long winded and took too long. Even after the Cairngorm Board radically downsized and modified its original plans for Lurcher's, no one wanted to know or were even prepared to meet half way.

The plans were sensitively modified, altering the proposed entry to the foot of Lurchers to a single track to be used only by a dedicated bus service with no other vehicles and car parks allowed. The only building was also to have a low profile with essential toilets, first aid provision and a simple refreshment area. The proposed chairlift was also altered to become a ski tow, also with a much lower visual profile There would be minimum use of snow fencing and every effort was to made to satisfy the conservationist.

The conservationists were winning the game and even at that stage, I hazarded the guess that many of them had never even walked on Cairngorm or stopped to consider the social significance of thousands of young people being stretched and tested on a small part of the winter mountain. They were just "anti" in principle. The public inquiries came and went, ideas were modified, plans were altered and shelved and still no decisions were made.

The Scottish Office shilly-shallied as Michael Forsythe, tried to find the best political horse to back. The Greens or Conservationists won the battle of Lurchers Gully. They were the popular movement of the time and their publicity machine made more noise.

At one point figures were released to show that 3,000 submissions had been made to the Scottish Office from the conservation people and only 150 from the skiing lobby. But, another poll showed that the public was equally divided. Many people on both sides of the debate were surprised that there was no compromise, no bartering, no meeting of minds between the two camps.

Twenty years ago the Chairlift Co., announced that it planned to challenge the establishment and sue the then Secretary of State for Scotland, Mr. Lang, for compensation following his refusal to allow limited development in Lurcher's. The company was seeking £100,000 which they said was the cost of investigating the feasibility of the proposed development. Tim Whittome, a spokesman, said that Cairngorm had been encouraged by the Scottish Office to make plans within the laid down guidelines and the change of mind at the eleventh hour had cost the company dearly and he mentioned £1 million in annual income.

The feeling of the pro-skiing lobby at the time in 1990 was bitter disappointment of course, but, with hindsight, the expectations of the skiing public in Scotland were already changing, they were looking further afield, to the Alps and beyond. Adam Watson when he wrote about the impact of environmental damage at Scottish ski centres he was appealing to the growing numbers of "Greens", and environmentalist. However, Adam was a realist and while he pointed out the dangers of too much development and in the wrong places, he also acknowledged that much of the polarisation was unnecessary. Many skiers were hill walkers and climbers in summer and had a lifelong care about wild life conservation. So too, some Conservationists or Greens were active skiers.

On one occasion in Aberdeen I was asked to speak at a meeting of concerned mountaineers, chaired by Adam Watson. I had been fairly vocal on the skiers point of view over the Lurcher's debate and expected to have a hard time. So deliberately I carried with me, my old climbing balaclava, my skiing bonnet and a safety hard hat, just to underline the fact that I had feet in all camps. I did have a hard time at that meeting but I'll bet my ski boots that the majority in that room had used car parks and ski lifts at some time in their lives and had helped to create erosion and unsightly scars with their boots, on the mountains they used for their playgrounds. As the verbal slings and arrows flew, I kept switched hats and managed to keep things jocular up to a point.

Damage Repairs

Talking about the damage being created by too many boots climbing the Cairngorms, I must quote a news item of 24th June 2010.

Cairngorm paths to get £720,000 repair boost

Nearly 60 miles of mountain paths in the Cairngorms will be repaired with the help of a £720,000 lottery windfall today. Constant use by walkers and mountaineers and the harsh climate have taken their toll of 17 upland paths which will be restored in the four year project. Some of the routes date as far back as the Middle Ages when they were used as droving roads to move cattle from east to the west. Damage has caused unsightly scars on the picturesque landscape and threatens important wildlife habitats. Repairs will be carried out by hand, with helicopters flying in materials to protect the terrain and minimise the disturbance to wildlife. Colin Mclean head of the Heritage Lottery Fund in Scotland said, "The stark beauty of Scotland's mountain heritage attracts an ever growing number of walkers, climbers and tourists each year. This a significant boom for our tourist economy, but we have to balance it with the conservation of our landscape and its flora and fauna so people can continue to enjoy it for years to come.

Now that is interesting and good news for our mountains. Those with sarcastic tendencies could say that they have not heard of any objections from the "greens" and the "anti everything" lobbies. Surely they should be objecting to so many walkers/climbers creating such damage and litter on our fragile mountains, all by their selfish actions.

Crunch Time

June 26th 1990 was the day of reckoning for the Lurchers saga. It was the day that Malcolm Rifkind, the then Scottish Secretary, dealt a major blow to the Highland Council's structure plan. The Tory minister was sometimes described as the cleverest minister in Margaret Thatcher's cabinet but prone to changing direction. He was immediately accused of using Lurcher's Gully as a political ploy. *"it fits the government's new enthusiasm for green policies",* as the leader article of the Scotsman said the following day. *"there are not many industries that thrive in the Highlands and from the very beginning skiing seemed to be the one that deserved maximum encouragement ... The threat it posed to the environment was not exactly on the same level as industrial pollution or poisonous waste".* That last point referred to the Scottish Secretary's leaning towards granting permission for toxic waste treatment and the dumping of nuclear waste in Scotland.

Not all press coverage was pro-development of the skiing industry and in 1985 the BBC Radio Scotland edition of "Taking Issue" the presenter Colin Bell tried hard to be provocative. He asked why anyone in their right mind should want to ski in Scotland with its *dreadful weather conditions, frequent snow shortages and long, long queues."*

Skiers have been asking themselves that same question for many, many years. But of course they did and still do, ski in Scotland.

Schizophrenia

Cairngorm became the main battle ground between opposing sides, because visually, it happened to be a very attractive mountain when seen from the Spey Valley. If it's first modest ski developments had happened in a less visible area, a hidden valley for instance, would there have been the same conflict? One Aberdeen Ski Club member in 1983 admitted that during the Lurcher's controversy, he had an oddly schizophrenic feeling.

As a member of Aberdeen SC he was of course counted as a supporter of the proposed development. But, as a member of the Cairngorm Mountaineering Club, he found he was assumed to be a dedicated opponent. Duncan MacRae said, that much of the time, the two sides seemed poles apart, when in fact they were both users of the same environment. One side spoke of "spoilation", a favoured word of the conservationists, of any type of mountain development. For them, even bridges and bothies were suspect; ski lifts and toilets should be verboten. *"The anti-everything lobby required that the use of our mountains, be limited to a few people, in effect, a small group of privileged mountain lovers, themselves."* His words, not mine.

He referred to the passage of the boots of climbers on the main route to Lochnagar, and the track between Cairngorm and Ben Macdui, on the high plateau. This is where erosion has become a huge problem, erosion from too many climbing boots. On Lochnagar, construction is still taking place to maintain paths and drainage channels on the heavily used route by the Ladder to the boulder fields on the summit ridge. Elsewhere, the efforts of the John Muir Trust are valued because of the work they sponsor, in repairing and creating mountain foot paths. The most recent example of their conservation work is on Schiehallion, by Kinloch Rannoch. The old wide and wandering muddy tracks up to the higher boulder fields, were by-passed with well drained paths. The heavy scarring of the past, is growing over, and the Hill of the Fairies looks so much more beautiful today. Duncan MacRae's point was that it was purely a matter of numbers on the hills, not whether they were skiers, or climbers. He wrote his piece in the Aberdeen Ski Club annual journal of 1983 and it was printed on the page next to a major article by Adam Watson. It was all a hotly debated subject then, and for some, it still is.

Astonishing Arrogance

The Cairngorm Chairlift Company was caught in the middle. The skiing community wanted more ski lifts, as queues became depressingly longer, and the company made a plea for the skiing fraternity to be more vocal and proactive in their opposition to the anti everything movement. In 1989 the International Union of Alpine Associations (UIAA) held a major conference at Glenmore Lodge, by Aviemore. The ski lift company wasn't invited but did invite delegates of the Mountain Protection Commission to visit the area. This was part of the policy to establish contact with all groups concerned about development into Lurcher's Gully.

Four UIAA members did make time for a short meeting on Cairngorm and the Cairngorm Chairlift Company explained why Lurcher's was so important for the completion of the existing ski area, within the boundaries set thirty years before. Shortly after this meeting the UIAA issued a statement which indicated that mountaineering organisations "simply wished all mountains to be reserved for climbers". This was an astonishing statement and a bitter pill for skiers in general. The Scottish skiing movement and the early developments were built by climbers who saw downhill skiing as another, equally valid way of enjoying the mountains in winter. Tim Whittome of the Chairlift Company reiterated, *"Downhill skiing in Scotland brings great pleasure to thousands in winter, yet only occupies one half of one percent of the mountain area over 2,000 feet. It also brings the possibility of year round employment. It seems a great pity that one group of mountain users effectively have sole use of Scotland's mountains."*

Exhaustion

The constant arguing about Lurcher's Gully went on and on for 25 years. First Roger Smith, the Chairman of the Scottish Wild Land Group said, *"Buy the Cairngorms to save them"*, and the daily columns in the national press were filled with prominent voices urging for and against. Roger and Sandy Cousins of the Mountaineering Council of Scotland both crossed swords with me in print. Everyone had a view, politicians pontificated but did not decide and conservationists moaned continuously about the vandalism taking place. Scientist had their say, local government people had their say, loud and biased voices were heard, vested interests denied being "hungry developers". It went on and on. Newspapers recorded every shade of opinion. So called National Planning Guidelines blurred the picture and confused the public. It was all horribly messy.

Incredibly, as all the turmoil was going on at Cairngorm, even more planning permission was being granted by Highland Regional Council for two other possible ski developments near the A9 south of Aviemore. The owner of the Drumochter Estate in 1987 ruled out a proposal by Rudi Prochaska a pioneer ski instructor in the village, in favour of a proposal by a consortium of local businessmen called the Drumochter Ski Development Group. Then came the small print in the Highland Council Plan! *"The area is included in the national planning guidelines for skiing development as a secondary development area with a general presumption in favour of development. But, the proposals are opposed by the Nature Conservancy Council, the Scottish Wildlife Trust and the Scottish Wild Land Group."*

Some say today that these bodies should now be examined to see if they are moving with the times. Their strident voices have been heard over the years and some folk think they are out of step. The questions must be asked because other bodies, trusts, groups, councils, associations and quangos are coming under the microscope today.

Let's look at what is happening to SNH, the Scottish Natural Heritage, which has been *"living beyond its means"* for many years. George Reid the last presiding officer at Holyrood, pulled few punches in his damning report delivered in 2010. His first target was the ruling council, which had 87 members and needed to be replaced by a 15-strong board. He also called for more co-operation between similar bodies such as Historic Scotland. A former Board member of SNH did write to Mr Reid admitting the there had been, *"too much sentiment and not enough financial sense"* and the view was that the old governance structure was, *"rooted in the 1930's"* while the unwieldy management structure included 187 trustees.

So, it would seem that the once respected body could do with some "tightening up" and with it, perhaps the Cairngorm National Park and a flock of other well meaning groups, trusts and quangos. Let's blow fresh winds through old conventions. The Drumochter ski plans never saw the light of day.

Glenshee also had its share of conflict but the Dundee consortium, with Manager David Patterson was able to push ahead with developments into adjoining valleys, essentially hidden valleys. They had battles to win against planning authority lethargy and occasional bad press and also input from the anti-brigade. But, Glenshee did develop to have the largest number of lift and chair installations and, to live within its budget. But then thankfully, Glenshee was not and, is not managed by a quango!

Beware

You may just have noted my dislike of negative people, the anti-everything brigades, too many cooks and, I am puzzled about the place of quangos in our society. Time has moved on in outdoor recreational terms. More of us use the "great outdoors" but in many more different ways. New sports are mushrooming, more facilities are opening up for us but sadly, the *"negatives"* still lurk in dark places

There were echoes of intolerance and negative thinking in a more recent incident in Highland Perthshire. It wasn't an environmental issue, but it was aimed at stopping a major cycling event, established in 2007, from taking place. In May 2009 a maverick member of an action group called ACRE, (Anti Closed Road Events) sabotaged the entire Etape Caledonia cycle event involving more than 3,500 cyclist. He, or she, sprinkled a large number of common tacks on sections of the road by the steepest and fastest sections, causing chaos and damage, major interruption, some injury and great danger of injury for the hundreds who had punctures at downhill speed!

Etape Caledonia

The 81 mile route is from Pitlochry, by Tummel and Loch Rannoch, round that loch, back by the Schiehallion hill road and down to the Tay Valley and

Glen Lyon, doubling back by Aberfeldy and then to Pitlochry by back roads. As the cavalcade of cyclists progress, the roads are immediately re-opened with major sections being opened by midday. The brief closures are necessary for obvious safety reasons and for just a few hours early on one Sunday each May. As soon as the cyclists pass, the roads reopen, and the police make arrangements for emergency vehicles to have access at all times.

I highlighted that story at the time because I had helped to run a water and feeding station at the event and was rewarded by the great atmosphere, the courtesy and thanks of the thousands of participants on the day. It is an exciting and major sporting occasion. So who are the complainers and those who are prepared to sabotage it? One person was suspected of the crime and was questioned at length but lack of evidence caused the case to be dropped by the Police, for the moment. Meanwhile, suspicions still exist and the investigation does continue.

Footnote:
Just as the 2010 Etape ended successfully, a spectator said to me, *"did you hear the guilty person last year had a collaborator"*. I said no, and he said, *"Oh yes, he was heard saying, "You tack the high road and I'll tack the low road"*. Sorry! I just couldn't resist that one. Sadly in 2011 the tack spreaders were at it again but their attempts to spoil the magnificent day for 5000 cyclists was foiled by vigilant supporters. I think I have underlined my dislike of the negative folk in society and this was another serious instance of the anti brigade at work. Shame on them!

The ACRE protestors insist that citizens should have public roads open at all times. That is preferable of course but there are many closed roads events, throughout Europe and through the centres of our own capital cities when marathons are run, or for military parades and for Hogmany celebrations. Now Glasgow is planning road closures for a major cycle event. On the Continent many major cycle events call for closed roads and the Tour de France is just one major example. The tourist spin off from these international events is incalculable.

What was interesting was the public reaction to the road closures in

Perthshire. A few protested and some small businesses did suffer from loss of income, but not too many or too much. The majority however, make special efforts to cater for the thousands of competitors and their families and supporters. Churches change times for morning services. Hotels and bed and breakfast establishments are full and over flowing and they bring forward morning breakfast times to accommodate the cyclists with the very early start time. While some lose out, it is estimated that the tourist inflow from that weekend alone in 2009, brought in £600,000 and that figure topped one million in 2010 when over 4000 cyclists took part with an equal number, and more, of camp followers.

One businessman did complain in 2008 that he lost £6000 in income over the few hours of road closure one Sunday in May. A contributor to the popular Highland Perthshire "Comment" magazine, queried that statistic and asked, *"What business you may ask, was he running for a few hours early on one Sunday morning, not in a village, but by a quiet rural road? Was the complainant being disingenuous or was it just exaggeration?"* The paper went on, *"Today, cycling is the fastest growing outdoor sport in the country and Highland Perthshire is a very safe place to hold mass events. The interest in the sport mushrooms and in the last few years several local cycle events have started up, involving young people. Scotland is cycling"* and *Highland Perthshire is the epicentre."*

The hot news is that Glasgow is to bid to bring the "Grande Depart" of the Tour de France, to Scotland to round off the coming of the Ryder Cup and the Commonwealth Games both coming to Scotland in 2014. Now that should really upset the ACRE campaigners!

Forward in time

The Golden days of Scottish skiing have come and gone as we all move into a new century. The first Aviemore Centre opened in 1966 has gone, to be replaced by the new resort centre. Where Cairngorm was once called the "Chairlift Company" it is now "Cairngorm Mountain Ltd" and it has a mountain railway to tempt lazy tourists to look at the mountains ... but not to walk on them. Glencoe, the cradle of Scottish skiing, has also moved into the 21st century and has become "Glencoe Mountain Resort". Glenshee is still called Glenshee despite being in Glen Clunie ... that was just an anomaly!

All the ski centres have diversified in one way or another. The Lecht has floodlit plastic slope sessions and a kart racing circuit, quad bikes and mountain bike tracks while Nevis Range with its gondola is a great summer attraction for tourists and a mecca for mountain bikers. Aonach Mor has hosted Mountain Bike World Cup events every year since 2002 and the World Championships in 2007. So yes, Scotland still skis whenever it can. The sport is more sophisticated, our expectations are higher. Our skiers still compete and Scots do figure largely in British Teams. So, it was quite a journey!

On your bike

Acknowledgements

My thanks are due to the late Alexander S. Burns RSW who in the 1960s drew the many cartoons used in this book. He contributed his work to many Ski Club publications at that time and captured the scenes of early skiing. He was head of Art at Hazelhead Academy in Aberdeen and was a very prominent water colourist. He and his family were enthusiastic early members of the Ski Club.

I am grateful to Paul Satney of Kincraig and Aviemore Photography for the use of his "Naked Skier" which was a best selling postcard for many years. And, to David Duncan my oldest skiing companion for his photograph used on the front cover.

So too the many friends I have enjoyed skiing with over many years and of course my loved ones and family for support.